3⁰⁰

# AGUIRRE

# Aguirre

*The Re-Creation of a Sixteenth-Century Journey*
*Across South America*

## Stephen Minta

JONATHAN CAPE
LONDON

First published 1993

1 3 5 7 9 10 8 6 4 2

© Stephen Minta 1993

Stephen Minta has asserted his right under
the Copyright, Designs and Patents Act, 1988
to be identified as the author of this work

First published in the United Kingdom in 1993 by
Jonathan Cape
Random House, 20 Vauxhall Bridge Road, London SW1V 2SA

Random House Australia (Pty) Limited
20 Alfred Street, Milsons Point, Sydney,
New South Wales 2061, Australia

Random House New Zealand Limited
18 Poland Road, Glenfield
Auckland 10, New Zealand

Random House South Africa (Pty) Limited
PO Box 337, Bergvlei, South Africa

Random House UK Limited Reg. No. 954009

A CIP catalogue record for this book
is available from the British Library

Map © Malcolm Porter 1993

ISBN 0-224-02470-1

Typeset in Linotronic Bembo by
SX Composing Limited, Rayleigh, Essex
Printed and bound in Great Britain by
Mackays of Chatham plc, Chatham, Kent

# ACKNOWLEDGMENTS

CONTRARY TO popular belief, those who travel are more dependent than those who stay at home, and they incur more obligations.

From among the many who gave their time, encouragement, or hospitality, I should like to thank: (in South America) Jean Preston, Pedro Bacalla (Molinopampa), Alberto Mazarro, SJ, Alejandro Repullés, SJ, Rebecca and Steve Finamore; (in England) Lewis Taylor, Peter Rycraft, Sid Bradley, Simon Sweeney, and Susan Kellerman; (in Spain) Mikel and Agustín Elorza, Tonina Deias, Purita Urbina and the staff of the Public Library of Elizondo (Navarre).

Finally, my thanks to Anthony Gaff and Karen Lewis, who helped to shape this book in its early stages; and to Anne Newman, as careful and considerate an editor as any writer could hope for.

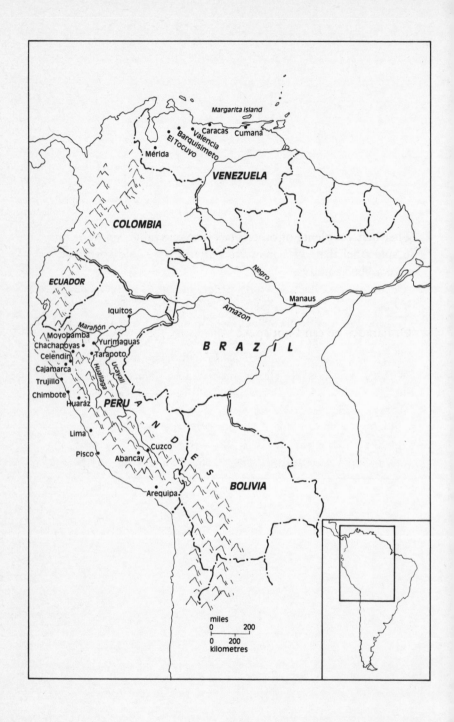

miles
0            200

0     200
kilometres

'Ther ben yet plente of other places so delectable, so swete and so spyrytuel that, yf a man were therin, he shold saye that it were a very paradys.'

William Caxton, *Mirrour of the World*

'Of Paradys ne can I not speken propurly, for I was not there.'

*The Travels of Sir John Mandeville*

# ONE

THE BODY, too, has a memory, even in this valley of ghosts. It recalls small, fleeting things, directly and without mediation, before the mind can name them or fix their place in time. The giddiness of arrival, the sickness in the lungs, and the swaying sensation, as if it was the sea and not the land under your feet – for the valley of Cuzco is one of the high places of the world.

> And when our father, the Sun, had made manifest his will to his two children, he bade them farewell. They left Titicaca and travelled northwards, and, wherever they stopped along the way, they thrust the golden wand into the earth, but it never sank in. And so they reached a small rest-house seven or eight leagues south of this city. Today it is called Pacárec Tampu, the Inn of the Dawn. The Inca gave it this name because he set out from here about daybreak . . . [and] its inhabitants to this day boast greatly of its name, because the first Inca bestowed it. From this place he and his wife, our queen, came to the valley of Cuzco, which was then a wilderness.

Many people still come to Cuzco, though fewer each year, now that the talk everywhere in Peru is of civil war. The easiest way is to fly down from Lima, a long way to the north-west. But you can still make the approach overland, like the first of the Incas, from Lake Titicaca and Bolivia in the south. By train it might be dangerous, for the line is often attacked. And by road it would be long and difficult, especially if you wanted to see Paccaritambo, the Inn of the Dawn.

But Paccaritambo is hardly worth the journey. Few now would boast of its name. It belongs to the desolation of a mountain twilight, rather than the gorgeous promise of an Andean sunrise, and it lies, like so many places here, on a rough track that leads nowhere, isolated and in wilderness.

Under the Incas, the wilderness of the Cuzco valley became the heart of the largest empire ever seen in the native Americas. A landscape of wind and rock transformed for a few generations, until the coming of the Europeans returned it to silence and chaos. There was a stone in the Greek temple at Delphi which marked the middle point of earth, the navel, centre of all that was known or worth knowing. Cuzco's name, too, meant navel and the city controlled the empire with such precision that an Inca ruler claimed 'there could not be a leaf of a tree moved without his will and authority'.

As the first Inca travelled north towards Cuzco, in the creation story told by the chronicler Garcilaso, he carried with him the golden wand symbolising fertility, a gift from his father the Sun. The Sun told him that a new kingdom would be born at the point where the wand sank into the earth; and the valley of Cuzco turned out to be that promised land, a place where an empire would be built on the power of maize and potatoes.

Even today, Cuzco doesn't sprawl. It has kept its figure, disciplined by tradition and geography. If you stand above the city and look down from the ruins of the Inca fortress of Sacsayhuaman, you can see how neatly it occupies a space of level ground, sometimes coming to a halt only a few feet from canyons so deep you cannot see to the bottom.

The city is isolated. There is nothing beyond it except the treeless slopes of the Andes. No people, few animals or birds. A twentieth-century French historian has called this a land of eternal autumn. Variations in faded brown; dry stunted grasses coloured only by the passing clouds. The Incas told themselves that history began here and, a little while before the Spanish came, when 'fearful comets appeared in the sky', the wise men of the Inca state suspected that it might end here too.

Now Cuzco's vast central square is dominated by Christian buildings, the massive blocks of Inca stone subdued under the weight of European tradition. The Cathedral and the Jesuit Church compete in Christian pride, where once the mummified bodies of the Inca rulers were paraded on feast-days, honoured as if still alive, as if there were no end to the world and death was only a series of unavoidable absences.

This is a city where you can feel the pain of oblivion. Few tribes or nations have been so deeply seduced by the past as the Incas, or have cared so much about preserving it. The professional historian of the Inca state, the *quipucamayoc*, could sing the entire imperial story from memory; and he remembered it diligently, since failure to do so was punishable by death. But though the Incas did all in their power to keep the story alive, through painting, dance and epic song, they never invented a system of writing which might have passed on all that they thought and felt to the unimaginable time when the empire would be no more. We were luckier in Europe; for Homer himself might have been no more than a name to us, but for that magical moment when the Phoenicians passed on to the Greeks the secret of their alphabet.

We know many things about the Incas. They practised the sacrifice of human beings, for example. They also practised ideas of social responsibility that can still intrigue us: if a man stole, he was punished severely, but if he stole because he was in need, then the state official in charge of his welfare was punished instead. They carried sexual humiliation to the level of state ritual: when a victory was won over another tribe, the vanquished leader was paraded naked through the streets of Cuzco on a litter for all to see. And they had comprehensive views on taxation: the poorest subjects of the empire, in the absence of any other source of wealth, were required to furnish a tribute of lice, so many per head of population, a kind of community charge to demonstrate that the duties and benefits of empire were for all to share.

3

But knowing all these things about the Incas and a thousand others, brings us no closer to what they thought of life or death or sexuality or their place in the world, though we might guess, perhaps, how they felt about the burdens of the louse-tax.

When the Spanish conquerors first saw Cuzco in the 1530s, it seemed to them a city of prodigious size. It was cosmopolitan, filled with Indians from all over the empire. But Francisco Pizarro, the new lord of Peru, quickly decided that the city could never be the capital of a new empire. Far from the sea and far from Europe, Cuzco began a long period of decline in favour of the new Spanish settlement at Lima. In the seventeenth century it was still rich and led a great school of colonial painting that is one of the delights of the modern city. But it never again had power in Peru.

Only romantically reinvented, brought back to life by a nation desperate for an image of success, have the Incas prospered. While their descendants are routinely despised on the streets of Lima, the great Incas themselves now offer an afterglow of unity to the fractured world of post-colonial Peru. A recent opinion poll taken among school-children in the major cities asked the question: 'When was the happiest time in the history of Peru?' During the time of the Incas, replied 84.1 per cent; while from Cuzco itself the message was that only eight students in a hundred could imagine happiness anywhere outside the old empire which had once made their city the centre of the world.

At a cross-over point between Indian and European culture lies the story of El Dorado. The myth of the gilded man was an entirely Indian invention, but the struggle to turn it into reality was an obsession of the Europeans alone. The Indians sometimes helped and sometimes hindered the fulfilment of this obsession. They fought with the Spanish and cooked their meals, built their boats, and suffered from their diseases, but we seldom hear much about them. The *conquistadores* had come to

4

change the way the New World was run and they had no interest in the past. So, in the writings of most of the chroniclers, there were only good Indians and bad Indians, according to how they adapted to the dreams of the conquerors; just as the landscape of Peru, through Spanish eyes, is only a succession of rich valleys and troublesome mountains.

El Dorado started life as a person, who may once have been real, and ended as a country, which was no more than a mirage.

The Indian myth, as it was told to the *conquistador* Sebastián de Benalcázar, was about a prince or priest who covered his body with resin before bathing in a sacred lake. Gold offerings were thrown into the lake, from which the prince emerges as a 'gilded man', the golden idol whose name the Europeans will later transfer to a land of the imagination where all will be touched by gold.

In the late 1550s, a Basque adventurer named Lope de Aguirre set out from Cuzco in search of El Dorado. There was nothing unusual in that; indeed, it was almost a commonplace. In those days, as the chronicler Garcilaso says, 'any Spaniard, even a poor soldier, thought all Peru together too little for himself alone'.

Besides, for a penniless *hidalgo*, there was nowhere else to go. It was over twenty-five years since the Spanish had seized Peru from the Incas. Most of the Indians had been overcome. A time of civil war among the Spaniards had come and gone, and the age of the fighting man was drawing to a close. Soon the title of *conquistador* would ring only in memory, as the Spanish bureaucrats worked to usher in what one historian has called 'the sad tranquillity of colonial Peru'. The expedition on which Lope de Aguirre was embarked was a final chance, the greatest of them all.

El Dorado. A banal illusion, now that all the world is known. For a long time we have lived with the virtual certainty that there is nothing on earth left to discover. El Dorado is now only the tarnished promise of beaches in the sun, or the abstract routine of the lottery or the football pools.

5

But in the early years of the sixteenth century, it was still possible to believe that somewhere, in a jungle clearing or on the stony altiplano, there was a place that would redeem a lifetime of hardship. Old men like Francisco Pizarro, illegitimate, illiterate, from one of the most backward parts of Spain, had lived to see 225 llama-loads of gold and silver brought at his command from the Inca temple in Cuzco. So why should El Dorado be false?

The moment of opportunity opened wide and closed again within a generation. F. Scott Fitzgerald catches its fleeting, unrepeatable magic in a famous passage at the end of *The Great Gatsby*. As he gazes on Gatsby's house, Nick Carraway relives the sudden flowering of a New World through virgin eyes: 'For a transitory enchanted moment', he imagines, 'man must have held his breath in the presence of this continent, face to face for the last time in history with something commensurate to his capacity for wonder.'

And what is the promise of El Dorado, if not precisely that? But the frontier is quickly shifting, and Lope de Aguirre's own search begins on one side to end on the other. In a great journey across South America, he proceeds from the wonder of the New World and its seemingly endless capacity for revelation to the bitter certainty that El Dorado is passing even as it is pursued. Only rarely can we guess from the chroniclers what Aguirre truly thought about his adventure, but if you can measure the depth of a man's belief by the vastness of his disappointment, then Aguirre was once a passionate believer.

You can feel the empty spaces closing as you read the great history of the Incas by Garcilaso. In a few lines he takes away possibilities which the authority of Aristotle had held open for 2,000 years. Aristotle had declared that 'the lands beyond the tropics are uninhabitable', that there were only two habitable sectors of the earth's surface, for everything else was too hot or too cold. But Garcilaso was a man of the New World; he had seen for himself and knew that Aristotle lied:

I myself was born in the torrid zone, in Cuzco, and was

brought up there until I was twenty, and . . . I have been in the temperate zone to the south beyond the Tropic of Capricorn . . . [and] passed through the torrid zone from one side to the other . . . so that I can assert that the torrid zone is habitable as well as the temperate.

Garcilaso's attitude is rational, sceptical, and unitary:

I will say at the outset that there is only one world, and although we speak of the Old World and the New, this is because the latter was lately discovered by us, and not because there are two. And to those who still imagine there are many, there is no answer except that they may remain in their heretical imaginings till they are undeceived in hell.

So there is only one world, with no space left for dragons or unicorns or El Dorado.

The existence of El Dorado was so little doubted for a time that people drew maps of it. There's a famous one with a coastline that looks like the coast of southern England near the Isle of Wight. Ships are sailing into harbour before a walled city topped with spires and turrets; it's reassuring and domesticated.

This domestication is an essential part of the myth. The promised land was to be a fabulous one, certainly, of unheard wealth and wonder. But it would also be a place where you could settle down. The rough men who left Peru with Aguirre wanted nothing but that. They wanted, in a phrase that recurs over and over again in the chroniclers, 'to discover and settle' (*descubrir y poblar*). It's an old paradox, as old as travel itself: the adventurers yearning for peace and security, while those settled back at home dream of excitement and new horizons.

But if the story of some ancient custom among the Chibcha tribes of the Andes lies at the origin of El Dorado, the belief in its existence was given renewed support by an account that comes from a different area altogether. As the Europeans began to make themselves at home in the Andes, thoughts turned to

7

the much larger spaces of the jungle and the stories of a gigantic river.

So in the 1550s, a tale was often related about an Indian leader called Viaruzo, who came from a long way to the east, in what is now Brazil. It was said that he had left his homeland with an army of 13-14,000 warriors. They brought 1,500 canoes, 'a sort of small boat made out of a single piece, in which the Indians travel by river and even by sea', as one of the chroniclers explains. Armed with bows and arrows, and improbably accompanied by two Portuguese who spoke their language, the Indians ascended the Amazon in search of better land, or, in the words of one of the wilder chroniclers, 'to satiate their accursed stomachs with human flesh'.

After some weeks they came upon a great lake in an area described variously as lying in a broad plain or at the foot of high treeless cliffs. They found large Indian communities living there, so numerous that 'the Brazilians remained astounded and terrified to see so many of them'. The Brazilians entered the lagoon in their canoes and the local people took up arms against them.

A great naval battle ensued and more than 10,000 of the Brazilians were killed or taken prisoner. Viaruzo withdrew, set up some of his men in a small village, and then pressed on with the rest up the Amazon, encountering many other Indian settlements but anxious now, we are told, no longer to conquer, but simply to discover the end of the river and return home.

Fourteen years after they had first set out from eastern Brazil, they struggled into an area of Peru occupied by a tribe the Spanish called the Motilones ('people who shave their heads'), an area that was under the control of the Spanish frontier town of Santiago de Muyobamba (modern Moyobamba). The exhausted Brazilians, without either of their Portuguese companions, both of whom had died on the river, were quickly taken prisoner and brought before the Spanish authorities.

For whatever reasons, the Brazilians said that they had seen on their journey a land richer than all Peru, with such quantities of gold and silver as could not be imagined. The story fell on willing ears and Viaruzo, along with half-a-dozen others, was brought to Lima where he repeated his tale before the greatest officer of the land, the marquis of Cañete, Third Viceroy of Peru.

Viaruzo had a bracelet and 'the hearts of men were moved by the desire to see and possess it'; (one of the chroniclers uses the verb *conquistar*: 'to conquer it'). So, on the basis of the story and the single bracelet, the Viceroy, 'as a good servant of His Majesty, and eager that, in his time, another new Peru should be discovered', decided to send out an expedition into the jungle in search of the riches of which the Indians had spoken. It was this expedition that Aguirre came down from Cuzco to join.

Lope de Aguirre was born in Spain, some time between 1511 and 1516. He came from the Basque country, from the town of Oñate, now in the province of Guipúzcoa. Oñate lies south of the town of Bergara, about twenty miles from the sea. In Basque its name means 'place abounding in hills'; the country is good for sheep, but difficult to farm, and emigration has always been part of the pattern of local life.

Poverty no doubt was the reason for Aguirre's initial journey across the Atlantic. In his twenties, he joined the great floodtide heading for the New World; and, at some point, perhaps towards the end of 1534, he arrived in Cartagena de Indias, the slave-trading port on the Colombian coast. Then, for a quarter of a century, he lived and fought in South America, gaining nothing and leaving hardly a trace.

A hostile chronicler – though, as we shall see, they are all hostile to him – gives us a picture of Aguirre in the 1550s: he was 'of medium height, unprepossessing, lame, a great talker and curser, not to say a renegade, with a half-caste (*mestiza*) daughter who was not at all bad-looking'. And the account continues: 'I saw this Lope de Aguirre many times . . . sitting in a Basque tailor's shop, and when he started to talk the whole street was engulfed in the sound of his voice.'

Unattractive, overbearing, even a little ridiculous – there is no one who knew Aguirre who ever wrote a good word about

9

him. But somewhere in the course of his long journey across South America, Aguirre the boisterous, common man turns into a monster of unusual interest. He becomes a rebel and a traitor, winning official recognition at last. And when he dies, a proclamation is issued requiring that: 'Wherever the said Lope de Aguirre may have left dwelling houses, these should be levelled to the ground, that no trace or memory of them should remain; and that when they have been so levelled, they should be ploughed over and strewn with salt.'

This was obliteration on the grand scale, more suited to the greatest rebels of the New World, like Francisco Pizarro's brother Gonzalo, whose houses suffered a similar fate after his death. And this is the fascination of Aguirre's story – the rise of the commonest of men, one who comes, at the very end of his life, to prowl upon the American stage.

Aguirre's journey was to take him across the whole width of the South American continent, from the Pacific to the Atlantic. But it would be a journey without a return. This would be no *Odyssey*; there would be no hero coming home to Ithaca or Argos, covered in glory with the pride of a job well done; merely a sense of loss, concealed for the most part beneath an overwhelming arrogance, and the hopelessness of a man who knows only the fate of always having to begin again.

The failure of the journey in Aguirre's eyes would not be personal but circumstantial and due to the land itself. Writing, more than half in madness, to the King of Spain after a terrible voyage down the Amazon, Aguirre says: 'Never allow another fleet to be sent to this unhappy river.' He had seen a world that swallows whatever comes near, one that denies, by its scale, a man's ability to believe in the value of his own actions. 'Even if one hundred thousand men went there', he says, 'none would escape, for there is nothing on the river except despair.'

Traditionally, Cuzco marks the beginning of Aguirre's journey. Strictly speaking, there is no evidence that he ever came here, but it's likely that he did. Francisco Vázquez says that 'he was so turbulent and bad-tempered that no town in

Peru could hold him'; that he had been taken prisoner in Cuzco on charges of sedition; and that he chose to go in search of El Dorado rather than be hanged. Most of this is doubtful, but it connects Aguirre with Cuzco and folk tradition has always insisted on the link.

In the early 1980s I lived high above Cuzco's central square, down an alleyway so narrow that passing pack animals would flatten you against the wall with their burdens. There was an old Indian woman who sold llama fodder from a tiny dark recess and at night half-wild dogs would gather to chew over the refuse of the day. The sun never reached down into the street and it smelled of urine and long decay.

Higher still, towards the last of the red-tiled houses, you come to the large retaining wall of Colcampata, the palace of the Inca Huascar (1525–1532). On the left side of the road there's a gateway and, if you turn in there and follow the path, you arrive at a private house. Many people will tell you that this house once belonged to Lope de Aguirre. It's a fine place, surrounded by eucalyptus trees and fragments of Inca stonework. Under the tropical sun there's a smell of burnt grass and dry earth, like the smell of Mediterranean fields in high summer. On the other side, where the land suddenly falls away, there's a school and beyond it the railway line to Machu Picchu.

I spent some time trying to unravel the story of this house; it's certainly had a share of history. Simón Bolívar, the Liberator of South America, stayed here during a triumphal swing through southern Peru in 1825. Of Aguirre, however, there was no sign. Finally, I went to see the curator of the departmental archives, but I waited until I knew I was about to leave Cuzco, as I had already guessed what he would say. 'I understand why you have come,' he told me wearily before I began, with a gesture that suggested a lifetime among the fading records of the past. 'I have been through all the sixteenth-century material. I have even', he went on, with the dry relish of professional pride, 'I have even been through it several times. And I can tell you that there is nothing to connect this city with Lope de Aguirre.

Nothing at all. And I can say more: I can tell you that I am not displeased with my findings, not displeased at all.'

So that was that. But it didn't matter. The search for Aguirre in its early stages should never be taken too seriously. There were dozens of people called Aguirre in the late Middle Ages, and even the incomplete records show that plenty of them were called Lope. There is a Lope de Aguirre who was twenty-four years old in 1510 and who appears as a steward to the Count of Oñate; and there's a carpenter called Lope de Aguirre who turns up on the island of Tenerife at about the same time. There is a Lope de Aguirre who leaves Seville for Cartagena in 1534. Another who is shipwrecked off Havana in 1538, on his way back to Spain from Peru. Another who appears in the shipping records as having left Spain for the New World in March 1539. He, or they, leave traces in Nicaragua, Honduras, and Panama, but nothing is certain. So, until one Lope de Aguirre makes himself more famous than all the others, we might be looking at different versions of the same man all over South America or at different people entirely.

It's possible, or quite likely, that the Lope de Aguirre we are looking for made the journey from Spain to the Indies more than once. All he tells us himself is that he spent twenty-four years in Peru and that, for most of the time, he lived as a fighting man.

The only story before the late 1550s about an Aguirre who might be the Aguirre of El Dorado is told by Garcilaso. It is a savage tale about a large party of soldiers who were on their way from Potosí in Upper Peru (now Bolivia) to explore the lands further south. It's a story that well illustrates the tensions which existed in Peru between the state officials, who were set on imposing Spanish law, and the original frontiersmen, who felt themselves to be above it.

The soldiers had impressed Indian porters to carry their belongings. This may not sound a very serious offence, but the Spanish crown was determined that the Indians of the New World would not be enslaved. The chief magistrate of Potosí went out to investigate and, like the policeman faced with a line of speeding motorists, he arrested the last as an example to all those who had gone before. The bad luck fell on someone called Aguirre; and the drama which followed would, if this were truly the Aguirre of El Dorado, explain a good deal about what was to happen later.

Aguirre was sentenced to two hundred lashes of the whip, to be delivered in public. Even for the time and place this was excessive, as the leading citizens of Potosí were quick to point out. Usually, in such cases, the victim could buy his way out with a fine. But Aguirre had no money and the magistrate was unyielding. Aguirre asked to be hanged, rather than whipped. The most the magistrate would offer was a week's delay in carrying out the sentence, which Aguirre refused, on the grounds that to spend a week meditating on a whipping one could not hope to escape was almost as bad as the thing itself.

So he was tied naked across an ass and driven around the town, while men stationed at various points lashed him as he went by, 'to the great regret', Garcilaso says, 'of Indians and Spaniards alike, who grieved to see such a cruel wrong so causelessly executed on a gentleman'. After all this, Aguirre, not surprisingly, decided not to accompany the expedition out of Potosí. He refused all help, 'saying that the only thing he needed for his comfort was to find death and to hasten its coming as much as possible'.

But then pain and despair gave way to the desire for revenge, and, thereafter, the story begins to resemble other frontier tales from around the world. Aguirre pursued, the magistrate fled. Aguirre always on foot, for he says that a man who has been whipped across an ass should never again ride a horse. They cover great distances, over a period, says Garcilaso, of three years and four months. They reach as far north as Lima, but finally come down to Cuzco where the contest would be settled.

At this point in the story Garcilaso brings in a personal note concerning his father's nephew, who came from Estremadura in Spain. The beleaguered magistrate was also from Estremadura. Nephew and magistrate were friends and the one warned the other: 'Everyone in Peru knows that Aguirre means to kill you.' The nephew offered to sleep in the house which the magistrate had taken opposite the Cathedral, but the magistrate chose his own precautions: 'He always wore a mail shirt under his doublet and carried a dagger and sword, though this was against his profession.' In any case, he didn't want people suggesting he was afraid, for 'Aguirre was a small man and ill-built', a description which, for all its vagueness, does not contradict what we know about the Aguirre of El Dorado.

One Monday, at noon, Aguirre entered the magistrate's house. Finding him asleep over a book, he stabbed him fatally in the right temple, then several times in the body, only without wounding him, on account of his coat of mail. He then left the house, discovered he had left his hat behind, coolly returned to pick it up, and then finally, it seems, lost his head.

In his panic he was taken in by some noblemen, whom Garcilaso also knew, and he spent forty days and nights in a pigsty, while the whole of Cuzco was in uproar. After the forty days and nights were up – the biblical echo inevitably makes one suspicious of the whole story – the noblemen dressed Aguirre as a black labourer. (Cuzco was an important slaving city, but, even so, this must have been a risky form of disguise.) They gave him a black coat, shaved his hair and beard, and dyed his face, neck, hands, and arms up to the elbow. They then all walked out of Cuzco together, past the guards at the entrance to the city, and Aguirre was free.

He went on to Huamanga (now Ayacucho), 'where he had a close relative, a rich and noble citizen who was one of the chief people there'. However, says Garcilaso, with his usual studied discretion, 'We do not mention his name here, because he had harboured a criminal in his house and succoured him in defiance of the royal justice.' All in all, the episode was, Garcilaso concludes, 'one of the most remarkable events of the time in Peru'.

The men who made the journey to the Indies in the 1530s had few things in common, except, perhaps, a desire to return home to Spain sooner or later. They came from every corner of the

Peninsula and from almost every social class, educational background, and occupation. There were men of the church, merchants, petty *hidalgos*, artisans, and peasants; notaries, accountants, and lawyers – all in great numbers; sailors, carpenters, coopers, swordsmiths, gunsmiths, barbers, trumpeters, and horseshoers. Some were literate, some were not. Few can have had much idea about what the New World would be like.

The expedition Aguirre joined was as varied as any other of the time. It attracted men from Castile and Navarre, León and Andalusia, Estremadura and the Basque country; from Portugal and Genoa, Madrid, Seville, Pamplona, Córdoba, Trujillo, Valencia, and San Sebastián. There were boat-builders and horse-tamers, notaries and priests, and at least a handful of men of high social standing, among them don Fernando de Guzmán, a young nobleman from Seville, and Juan de Guevara, a Knight Commander of the Order of St John.

But of all the men who went to try their luck on the Amazon, the one we know most about, apart from Aguirre himself, is the commander of the expedition: Pedro de Ursúa.

Ursúa was a *caballero hidalgo* from an old family of Navarre. His house still stands, much altered, in the Baztán valley, to the north of Pamplona, in the village of Arizkun. The Baztán is one of the most beautiful valleys in the Pyrenees and it controls one of the easiest passes across the mountains. In the Middle Ages the *baztaneses* grew rich on the traffic of pilgrims to Santiago de Compostela and merchants trading the long routes from France into Spain. Kings with their armies, Germans and Franks, Bretons and Normans, all passed down the valley. In its cosmopolitanism, wealth, and soft beauty it is far removed from Aguirre's home in Oñate. And yet Ursúa and Aguirre share one important thing: both came from the periphery of the new Spain that was to be centred increasingly on the power of Castile; both spoke Basque, as well as Spanish. To the Castilians of the Indies, the Basque was the absolute outsider, what the historian James Lockhart calls 'the very prototype of the foreigner'.

Not that Ursúa, as a *caballero hidalgo*, faced the same problems as Aguirre, nor, as far as we can tell, did he feel the same resentments. But his ancestral home in Arizkun is a long way from Valladolid or Madrid. It lies only seven miles from the French frontier, which allowed Aguirre, when his former commander was dead, to taunt him with being 'a Navarrese, or, to tell the truth, a Frenchman'. A singular form of abuse at the time, since France and Spain had by then been at war for half a century.

It's not easy to decide what Ursúa's contemporaries thought about him. That he was a good soldier is beyond doubt. He was a man of great experience and it's inconceivable that the Viceroy would have entrusted his Amazonian expedition to anyone but the best: he was handsome, in what might have been considered the prime of life, for he was thirty-three when the Viceroy gave him his command; a gentleman, of course; of medium height, reddish beard, genial in conversation. Garcilaso, who knew everyone of importance in Peru, says that he was someone 'of great goodness and virtue' and 'a very popular figure everywhere'.

Perhaps. But sometimes even the most fawning of the chroniclers have their doubts. According to Toribio de Ortiguera, for example, Ursúa was *adamado*, an adjective he obviously chooses with care, for *adamado* is a word with both positive senses ('elegant', 'refined') and less happy ones ('affected', 'effeminate'). It's an odd thing to say of the commander of an expedition into the jungle. All the chroniclers were well aware that Ursúa had the reputation of a womaniser. They try to deal with it in different ways, but all are agreed it was a major problem. Only Garcilaso can stand far enough away to find detachment: passion, after all, he says, 'has been the ruin of many great leaders in the history of the world'.

Pedro de Ursúa was young when he came to the New World. He arrived in Cartagena at the age of eighteen. From then on, like most other men in the Indies, he spent his life fighting. He fought the Tairona Indians in the Sierra Nevada de Santa Marta, in what is now Colombia. Later, he campaigned further south. He founded two new cities: Pamplona, after the capital of

Navarre, and Tudela, in memory of the 'Pearl of the Ebro', his mother's birthplace.

Some time in the mid-1550s, he had his crucial meeting with the newly appointed Viceroy of Peru, the marquis of Cañete. The Viceroy initially offered him a labour of Hercules: the job of putting down a rebellion by fugitive black slaves in the Panamanian Isthmus. The rebellion had made large areas of the Isthmus unsafe for travel. But, more than that, it was a challenge that could not be allowed to succeed. For it was already clear to the authorities that the future prosperity of the Indies depended on black slave-labour. Ursúa cleared the Isthmus after vicious jungle fighting. He delivered scores of prisoners who were thrown to wild dogs and torn to pieces, as a signal that here, at least, business was business.

Now, with his reputation made, but apparently not his fortune, Pedro de Ursúa 'came up' – as they always put it – to Peru. Up, because the prevailing wind on the west coast of South America blows from the south. This made the journey from Peru to the Isthmus an easy one, while sailing in the reverse direction was often difficult. Ursúa arrived in Lima at the end of 1558 to find himself leader of an expedition in search of El Dorado, as a reward 'for all he had done in the war and pacification of the black slaves'.

Did he himself think of it as a reward? One must imagine so. Unless he was simply approaching an age when, with nothing behind him but years of fighting, always tied to the service of greater men, he thought it was time to settle down and doubted if there would ever be a better chance. For the marquis of Cañete, on the other hand, there was much less at stake. There had been many expeditions in search of El Dorado. They were called *entradas* in Spanish, meaning entrances, an odd word, since logically we would think of them as exits. All the *entradas* had at least the secondary aim, and often the primary one, of getting the discontented out of Peru and into the great spaces beyond, from which, with luck, they would never return.

So if, by chance, Ursúa went on to discover some rich new land, the Viceroy could take the credit for sending him. But if, as seemed more likely, this was to be a journey without an end, then Ursúa and his men would find that out for themselves, and far from Lima. The Viceroy must have felt secure. But he was never to see the results of what he had set in motion. He died in September 1560, just ten days before Ursúa's expedition finally set sail. His death, they said in Lima, was hastened by rage and melancholia on receiving an insolent letter from the man sent to replace him. Not that his successor was any more fortunate. He ran a high-class brothel during his term of office and died at the hands of an assassin.

So the story begins. The Viceroy of Peru is in shadowy control. Pedro de Ursúa is his chosen commander. And somewhere, as yet so indistinct that we cannot tell whether we see him or his double, is Lope de Aguirre, the future renegade. As we skim the pages of the chronicle, before attempting the more treacherous path of interpretation, we come face to face with oppositions simple enough to be reassuring: Ursúa, handsome, at an age when he could still die the romantic hero; Aguirre, almost fifty years old, misshapen, possessed by an anonymous rancour and extravagant hope; Ursúa, the best of what generations of European knighthood could offer, the model of elegance allied to martial skill; Aguirre, lowly and unnoticed, the very dregs of the Old World, with apparently no future in the New.

'This traitor would sometimes say', writes Francisco Vázquez of Aguirre, 'that he already knew for certain that his soul could not be saved; and that, even while he was alive, he was sure he would burn in hell. And, since the raven could be no blacker than its wings, that he must needs commit acts of cruelty and wickedness by which the name of Aguirre would ring throughout the earth, even to the ninth heaven.'

I returned to Cuzco in April 1987 for the first time in five years. The city looked and smelled the same. It gave its old, familiar welcome, somewhere between pain and elation, as the altitude starves the brain of oxygen. But it was different, too. Like returning after many years to see old friends and finding that you remember them far, far better than they remember you. The city had turned in on itself. There were fewer foreigners about. It was a poorer, rougher place and there were more areas it was safer to avoid. The civil war which, five years before, had been no more than a troublesome rumour from the north, had spread a long way up and down the chain of the Andes. There were new and shifting frontiers that were hard to make out and dangerous to cross. It was not a very good time to set out on the trail of a sixteenth-century Basque adventurer, but, with hindsight, it was a better time than any of the years that followed.

I moved into a small hotel on the edge of the city. It was protected by a high wall and an Alsatian that dozed in the sun by day and barked into the silences of the night. It was the beginning of the dry season in the mountains, the Andean summer which comes at a time when it is already winter in the coastal cities. As Lima settles into the darkness, Cuzco is overwhelmed with light. But even in summer its shadows are cold. If you find yourself sitting with your head in the sun and your feet in the shade, you can feel the line that falls across your body and the odd sensation of being cut in two.

A single day can bring all the seasons of the year. Breathless spring mornings. The dry heat of high summer at midday. Messengers of autumn in the late afternoon, when clouds roll over the sun. And sudden winter after dark, as the city squares turn quiet and intimate and the frost begins to glitter on the cobblestones.

On a Monday morning, some weeks after I arrived, I crossed the city to meet an old friend. It was early and the grass in the hotel courtyard was still white, but the Alsatian had found the first rays of the sun and was already asleep. Three mules sidestepped the long road down to the main square, their backs steaming in the morning air. In the harsh light every outline is acutely traced; the dark, sculpted balconies overhanging the narrow streets, the massive stone gateways that open on to silent houses. The city is austere, imperial, even against the brightness of Indian dress and the comedy of a passing llama, bored as only a camel could be bored.

Out towards the bus station the road deteriorates. Trucks carrying the early crowds to work slithered around potholes, stirring up clouds of dust. The bus from Lima arrived, looking more animal than mechanical. It snorted, lifted itself heavily over a low bridge, then shook like a dog that's just come in from the rain. It was silent and everything around it was silent too. Passengers disembarked painfully, stretching brown arms and legs. A few white people gazed cautiously about, wondering what to do next. Children ran their fingers along the side of the bus, discovering patches of green metal beneath the grime. It's a long way by road from Lima.

The driver looked exhausted, disenchanted, as if there might be easier ways of earning a living after all. He walked over to an Indian woman who sat on the edge of the road, roasting guinea-pigs over an open fire. The bus driver bought two, put one in his pocket, began to chew on the other, and disappeared into the smoke and dust.

People were still coming down the steps of the bus. Suddenly, the stream of colours and shapes slowed, solidified, resolved itself into a familiar form. It's curious how surprised you can be to see someone you know in a strange place, even when the only reason you're there is to see them. Jane stood on the bottom step, blinked in the light, rubbed her eyes with tiredness. It was five years since we'd met. She'd been living in Central America, in the highlands of Guatemala. She looked much older and darker and her black hair was cropped almost to the skull. She laughed.

'Yes, I'm beginning to think I'm a boy too. I thought it would be good for the journey. Only no one told me the nights are so cold. I'd have frozen to death in the mountains without my sleeping bag.' Then she caught her reflection in a mirror across the street. 'And I've been thinking I need a hat. I'm going to look a hundred if I stay out in the sun much longer. But it's not just the sun either. Five years of rice and beans and nobody looks the same.'

20

We walked into the centre of the city, looking for something that wasn't rice and beans. We went into a restaurant and Jane set her pack down against the whitewashed wall. The room was cold and she shivered.

'Does it really never warm up here? Perhaps it's just that I haven't eaten for two days. I've never been able to eat on buses.' She eyed some ageing avocados behind a cracked pane of glass. She pointed at one, called it *aguacate*, which is the common word for it in Spanish. In Peru they call it *palta*, though, after the Quechua Indian word *paltay*.

An old man behind the counter looked at Jane for a moment, then turned to face her, magisterial, as if he'd suddenly found himself in front of a blackboard. '*No es aguacate, señora, es palta.*'

'Oh God, what a language.' Jane rolled her eyes. 'You know I've only just found out that *aguacates* means bollocks in Central America? It's a weird culture. I don't think they've got anything you can eat that's round and doesn't mean bollocks.'

Jane took out a pile of English newspapers from the top of her pack which I read while she breakfasted on avocados. There had been a general election in Britain and I looked up the results for places I knew. Dry columns of figures sketched out an unchanging landscape. The victors already sounded bored with their triumph; the vanquished had nothing left to say.

When Jane had finished eating we walked back towards the hotel so she could get some sleep. We crossed the main square. There were piles of sweaters and gloves and scarves for sale. Most visitors buy them as gifts for friends, then, after a night or two, keep them for themselves. We met a woman from California whom I knew. She sold bracelets and earrings on the square, which is an odd thing for a foreigner to do in a country as poor as Peru, but I liked her. She had rough, wiry hair tucked into an old flat cap. She was thin and she never had any money. As we talked she kept licking at tiny brown sores around her mouth.

'I haven't been home since Reagan got in,' she said to Jane, as if it was an award for good conduct or long service under fire.

At dawn the next day a large Peruvian man stepped out of the shower, which steamed like a geyser into the frosty air. He wore a towel around his waist that suggested more than it concealed. He began to tread his way, barefoot on the grass, back to his room. He saw me looking at him. At six in the morning perhaps he believed he had a right to privacy, a great beast with first claims at the watering hole. 'Are you watching me, *gringo*? You think I am too fat?'

It wasn't really that. His skin was smooth and had it been any paler, the mass of black hair would have made it look sickly. But it shone in the sun, like metal, precious red and gold.

'I will tell you something, *gringo*. If a man cannot see his penis when he wakes up in the morning, then maybe he's too fat, or maybe it's just that he's getting too old.'

At that moment Jane came up, also seeking privacy. She looked longingly at the shower. Cuzco had been without water for three days and she hadn't been able to wash since she arrived. Some people claimed that 'they' had done it, which usually meant the guerrillas of Sendero Luminoso. But most accepted the official explanation of incompetence and a worn-out system. Those with money had bought up all the mineral water in the city. Some were even taking baths in it, according to the local paper. Everyone else just waited.

'When we were children and we played around outside, my grandmother used to tell us we'd get so dirty we'd never be able to get the dirt out again. That's how I feel this morning. It's not much of a place, this hotel of yours. There's a French archaeologist with boyfriend troubles on one side of me. And then the desk clerk moved a woman in on the other side and at five o'clock there was a crowd of people down in the street shouting "Bring out the whore," and throwing stones at my window. You're sure this is the best you could find?'

We went to the main square to have breakfast. There's a famous café there called the Ayllu, which has all the fatigue and the quiet efficiency of a place where they've served the same food for twenty years. You can eat breakfast any time from eight in the morning until ten at night. They have an old gramophone, just a generation away from the wind-up ones, and a couple of dozen classical records that play all day long. The music sounds as thin as the air through which it moves. And another day's routines begin. Boys come by with the papers – first the Cuzco ones, later the Lima dailies – then more boys to shine shoes, young girls to beg or to sell postcards. Short, stumpy brown arms weave, challenge, and implore. Most visitors give freely. With a collapsing local currency and a hard dollar even charity is painless.

The morning was dull and there were few people about. The wind picked up old cigarette packets from the ground and pieces of paper from rubbish bins and pulled them in circles across the square. I remembered a time of bitter weather here, when for a week the snow line dropped lower and lower over the surrounding mountains. Then, one morning, I woke up and the whole city was under snow. The sun vanished for two weeks and the cold was everywhere. It followed you into cafés and private houses and nobody had heating. Still people went about in open shoes and sat for hours selling on street corners. Though the city was beautiful like this, it felt like one of the cruellest places on earth. I think it was then that I first considered writing the story of Lope de Aguirre.

# TWO

For the chroniclers who told the story, as for the soldiers who made it, this was always to be a tale of the Amazon. The journey from Cuzco down to the fringes of the jungle was a long and sometimes difficult one, but, by the 1560s, it was taken mostly through known territory and not dangerous. Beyond the limits of Spanish Peru, however, came the real jungle, about which the Europeans still knew very little.

Above all, it was the Amazon that amazed and terrified the invaders. Its tributaries made it the only means of travelling east of the Andes. The size of the river, the lack of food and inhabitants over vast stretches, the difficulty of tracing the river's course where, so often, it loses itself in swamps and lagoons, separating out between islands larger than some European countries – all this was a revelation.

It was also to be the setting for a power struggle in which, as a nineteenth-century English commentator wrote: 'All that is wildest, most romantic, most desperate, most appalling in the annals of Spanish enterprise seems to culminate in one wild orgie of madness and blood.'

A long time after we had left Cuzco, when the coolness of the mountains lay so far behind that it seemed to belong, like some lost ice age, to a period of prehistory, we were sitting in a café overlooking the river, in the jungle city of Iquitos. A coarse light filtered through the clouds to the yellow mass below. The city slept on, drenched in the warm rain and soft heat of late afternoon. I thought for the first time, surprisingly, since we had already been following it for many weeks: 'This is the Amazon.'

Still 2,000 miles from the sea, it's hard to believe that it's a river; because a river is movement, water taking its course from one point to another by the most efficient path. Here nothing moved, neither sky nor air nor water, all fixed since the beginning of time.

I think I understood something then of what the chroniclers were trying to say about the Amazon and its role in their lives. How they struggled to find their place in an arena that was so empty and open, full of fearsome possibilities; yet also enclosed, apparently unchanging. And how the drama they recorded reflected all this: the terrifying violence of Aguirre's story, reaching down to us like some old morality tale, full of elemental forces in which we no longer quite believe. But also the appalling sameness, the wretched familiarity, as if this was just a great family argument, suddenly gone out of control.

The difficulties of travel, people say, are mostly subjective. One man remembers the horrors of a journey that the next man recalls with affection. For some, travelling brings only hardship, loneliness, and the hostility of natives. But then H. A. Franck goes *Vagabonding Down the Andes*; and Arsène Isabelle, the Phileas Fogg of Le Havre, happily turns his back on his native land with an *Adieu, chaste Seine* and heads for Buenos Aires with a few smokeless candles in his pocket.

Peru can be no exception to this relativism. Even so, you don't find many people who think it's an easy place in which to go travelling. Unless, of course, you go by plane. And there is a great deal to be said for doing this. Away from the coast the air is often bright and clear and you can enjoy the grandeur in comfort, while at ground level you lose it so easily amid dirt and fatigue.

Overland travel in Peru has been a problem since the fall of the Inca empire. The Inca relay runners could pass a message from Cuzco to the coast in three days. The Incas maintained a network of roads through the Andes that was better than anything Peru has known since. They built their roads straight across the mountains, taking the line of least distance from one point to another. This meant that steep ascents were often made by steps cut into the rock, where the road would narrow to no more than a few feet. It was fine for a people who always travelled on foot, but it was disastrous for the Spanish horses, which quickly tired and frequently lost their shoes against the stone steps. The Spanish could not adapt the system to their own needs so it quickly fell into disrepair and journey times began to lengthen.

It could take two months on horseback to reach Lima from Cuzco at the beginning of the twentieth century, until the building of the Southern Railway at last joined Cuzco to the coast again. The historian Agustín de Zárate, who arrived in Peru in 1544, tells a characteristic story about road building in the time of the Inca Huayna Capac (1493-1525). The Inca had marched out of Cuzco to conquer the province of Quito, now in Ecuador:

> But such difficulties did he find in crossing the *sierra*, on account of the bad roads and great gorges and precipices, that the Indians decided to make him a new road by which to return when he had conquered the province. By the time he had won the victory, they had built a broad, smooth road over the whole range of the *sierra*, breaking and levelling the crags where necessary and filling the gorges with stones, sometimes to a depth of thirty or forty feet.

Zárate concludes his report of this miracle with a remark that confirms how quickly the road system fell to pieces after the Conquest:

> The road is still to be seen for a distance of five hundred leagues [about 1,700 miles], and it is said to have been so smooth when finished that a laden cart could be driven

over it. But since that time, owing to the wars both of Indians and Christians, the paving is broken in many places and gaps at dangerous points prevent the passage of travellers.

His final warning is still useful. There are few good paved roads in Peru. After heavy rain many tracks disappear and, even in the dry season, your path may be blocked by fallen rock, deep craters, or shifting sand. Only along the Pan-American highway that follows the Pacific coast, and in a few other places, can you be certain of finding a way through. Elsewhere, patience is everything.

On receiving command of the expedition to El Dorado, Pedro de Ursúa seems to have gone about his preparations in a logical way. From the beginning of 1559 he publicised the adventure all over Peru. He placed men he thought he could trust as recruiting agents in all the major cities: Pedro de Enciso in Lima, Juan de Aguirre in Chachapoyas, Lorenzo de Zalduendo in Cuzco. He established a base camp 600 miles north-west of Cuzco, in a place called Santa Cruz de Saposoa. And he spent months criss-crossing Peru, organising men and provisions, begging for funds, and trying to keep up morale among the soldiers who began to assemble in Santa Cruz.

Ursúa was an experienced leader, but this was to be the greatest expedition to appear on the Upper Amazon for 200 years. In the end, Ursúa took more than twice as many men as Pizarro had brought to conquer the whole of Peru. Inevitably, the organisation was very slow and it was to be eighteen months before the fleet finally moved out of its base camp and took to the river.

This delay had a number of consequences. Most important, it enabled the enemies of the Viceroy – and there were many – to plan their opposition to his project. They argued that since the first year of the Conquest Peru had known nothing but war, and that to assemble a force of fighting men on this scale and leave

27

them languishing for months on the edge of the jungle was asking for trouble. They were not far wrong. Ursúa was to face insubordination and desertion at the highest levels, and from those he trusted the most; and when the rebellious remnants of his expedition reached Venezuela in July 1561, they still formed an army of immense power, so that weeks of terror were to pass before the authorities were confident of engaging them.

Pressure on Ursúa grew from the very moment of his appointment. Powerful men insinuated that he was being used by the Viceroy; that the marquis of Cañete, angry at the rumours that the Spanish king was about to replace him, was trying to raise an army for treasonable purposes. The more time elapsed, the more Ursúa fell into debt. And the more endebted he became, the less able he was to call off his adventure once things started to go wrong.

Still, he did his best. He recognised that the expedition would need an enormous number of boats and one of his first priorities was to find the people with the skills to build them. Eventually he chose twenty-five men and together they went out into the country of the Motilones, beyond the frontier town of Moyobamba, to look for a suitable place for a shipyard.

At a bend in the river, with a fine stretch of smooth sand and plenty of good wood, they set up camp. The place was called Topesana by some, Capisana or Copesana by others: the disagreement must reflect the insignificance of the place. The chroniclers themselves were unsure where it was. Gonzalo de Zúñiga, who might have been expected to know, says it was twenty leagues [about seventy miles] from Santa Cruz. But other chroniclers say it was much closer, no more than four leagues away [about fifteen miles].

At any rate, there's no point in looking for Topesana today. Even the location of Santa Cruz de Saposoa is uncertain. Founded by the *conquistador* Pedro Ramiro, it had already vanished a century later, though it must have been somewhere on the Saposoa river, to the south of modern Tarapoto.

Ursúa left his carpenters and shipwrights in Topesana, with ten black slaves and many Indians who would cut and transport the wood. He then returned to the rumour house of Lima. Meanwhile, the marquis of Cañete, in one of those gestures that now seem absurd, but which were common at the time, had named his protégé Governor and Captain General of the River Amazon, from Santa Cruz to the Atlantic Ocean, with jurisdiction over all the Indians he might find along the way.

Jane sat in the hotel garden, with the Alsatian at her feet, and unfolded her map of Peru. The dog opened one eye, thought about raising its head, then lost interest and went back to sleep. The map was enormous. A great brown stain showed the mountains running all the way down from north to south. To the right of the mountains, our immediate destination: the huge white space reserved for the jungle. Here and there the space was filled in with tiny black names, where men far from home had left a record of their hopes and fears: Diamante Azul ('Blue Diamond'), Puerto Desengaño (Port Disappointment), Esperanza (Hope), Desprecio (Contempt), Las Hormigas (Ants); and, more often than any other name, the most beautiful word in the Spanish language, Soledad (Solitude).

The map shows clearly that there has never been an obvious route between Cuzco and the Saposoa river. If you place a ruler between the two areas it touches a few villages in the vicinity of Cuzco, but the mountains quickly give way to the jungle and, apart from an airstrip with the odd name of Puerto Inca, there is nothing for over 400 miles, until you reach the first settlements on the Huallaga river.

The route taken by travellers going north from Cuzco was always, until recently, along the path of the Inca highway described by Zárate. It follows the movement of the Andes, going west out of Cuzco towards the town of Abancay, before taking its course north through Jauja, Cerro de Pasco, Huánuco, Huamachuco, and Cajamarca. It takes you along one of the highest roads in the world, and, in the Indian towns of Huancavelica or Huancayo, there is the world's highest railway line for the descent to Lima and the Pacific. But the railway is now closed to passengers, and the road crosses through the poorest parts of Peru, the departments of Apurímac, Ayacucho, and Huancavelica, an area once freely called *la mancha india* ('the Indian stain'), now the very heart of the civil war.

'I might take that road to save my life,' said an old Cuzco friend, 'but for the sake of Lope de Aguirre, never. If you were unlucky, the Army would shoot you because you look like a journalist. And if you were very unlucky the guerrillas would shoot you because you look like a foreigner.'

Nowadays, to avoid the town of Ayacucho and the surrounding country, you need to go all the way to the coast. Then you can take the Pan-American highway north along the Pacific, before turning east and crossing back over the Andes for a second time, to rejoin the Inca highway further up and out of trouble. It's possible that Aguirre took a similar path, given the deterioration of the *sierra* highway in the late 1550s. But the chroniclers tell us nothing about this stage of his journey. Not even a chance remark on which to speculate.

Before we left for the coast, Jane and I went to see people and places I remembered. The mountains around Cuzco have never been at peace with their tourists, but they felt empty without them. The Inca citadel at Pisac, one of the finest sights in South America, was deserted and everywhere else, except for Machu Picchu, was the same. The Inca baths at Tambo Machay, the fortress temple of Ollantaytambo, Pikillakta, Tipón, Chinchero; places in Cuzco itself that once overflowed with people: the Café Literario, where the elegant came to be seen and take afternoon tea; Cuzco's pub, with its dartboard and sawdust and football scarves, once home to dozens of homesick British travellers.

At night the few foreigners there gathered around the old-fashioned ovens in the pizza houses. Sad-eyed musicians from Bolivia would come and sing their two songs of the mountains, before trudging out into the dark in the hope of a better audience. At that time there were more visitors from France

than anywhere else, either because the French were less well informed about what was happening in Peru or less troubled by it.
'*Ah, mais vous avez fait le chemin de l'Inca? J'savais pas que vous
étiez venus pour le trekking. Comme c'est folklorique, n'est-ce pas? Et
vous êtes toujours vivants?*'

Then, while it was still early, people would drift away and we
would walk back to our hotel, past the army post with its sign
in the window: 'God forgives, we don't.' And we'd play chess
in the deserted lounge until it was time for bed.

On a bright morning in early July we took the same bus that had
brought Jane to Cuzco and started on the long road through the
mountains. The bus crosses a pass so high that, if you were back
in Europe, you could reach out and touch the summit of the
Matterhorn. The villages of the southern *sierra* all look alike
to the outsider; low-walled houses, greying whitewashed
churches, dust, and stones. This is not a land of heroes: no
monuments; no names that live for ever more; no *morts pour la
patrie*. Peru had the first oil-well in Latin America. Tons of
nitrates and *guano*. Coal, phosphate, and natural gas. Yet the
countryside, for lack of energy, moves at the rhythm of a pre-
industrial age.

This rural world was governed until a generation ago by a
system known as *gamonalismo*: domination by a local landlord,
whose decisions were often arbitrary and invariably absolute.
Hugo Blanco, militant Trotskyist of the 1960s, son of a lawyer
and a peasant woman, remembered the dark side of the system
in his book *Land or Death*: the *gamonal* who printed his own
money, so that 'his' peasants could buy only from him; others
who marked their peasants with cattle-branding irons; another
who tied one of his subjects to a mango tree and flogged him for
an entire day as a lesson to all. Everywhere in the *sierra* are the
signs of past greed, past failure, and the hopelessness that we call
underdevelopment. A ragged, circular world, with no hope of
escape except to the shanty towns of the coast.

After Abancay the road forks one way to Andahuaylas and
Ayacucho, the other to Puquio, Nazca, and the sea. Just before

31

Nazca, the road crosses into the department of Ica, the mountains come to an end, and the desert begins.

As all school-children here will tell you, without waiting to be asked, Peru is really three separate countries. If you travel west to east, you start from a coastal strip that is almost total desert from the borders of Chile to the frontier with Ecuador. Parallel to this strip are the western and eastern ranges of the Andes with a high plateau in between that carries the natural lines of communication through the mountains. Further east still is the third Peru: the huge area of tropical rain forest. None of these three countries is particularly welcoming. According to a pre-Inca legend, no authority had ever felt the need to build prisons in Peru, since nature had already done all the work single-handed.

It is fashionable now to condemn the Spanish conquest, but it took imagination to persevere in the face of adverse initial impressions. When Pizarro first came to Peru he landed in the far north, at Tumbes. He took the Inca highway of the *llanos* across the desert towards the site of modern Lima. Then he turned east into the mountains and on to the central plateau to confront the Inca army outside the town of Cajamarca, 'the land of ice'. In a short time he had seen two of the three extremes of Peruvian geography.

At the town of Pisco the road reaches nearly to the sea, about 150 miles south of Lima. The coast here is one of the most desolate in the world. It is geologically young, like the Andes, and has few bays or ports. From the map you imagine a tropical paradise of white sand and sunshine, but this is a coast that is closed to the sea. The major cities along the Pacific turn their backs to it and, apart from a few fishing villages, you might as well be in Bolivia. Occasionally there's an oasis, where the land is irrigated by streams coming down from the mountains, but other than that you travel through true desert, windswept sand, cacti, and red rock.

For seven or eight months of the year this desert lies under a bank of fog. You don't see the sun for weeks at a time and the

Pacific looks grey, greyer than the English Channel in November, and sadder. A strange phenomenon called the *garúa* covers the land. People claim that this is Peruvian rain, but it provides no moisture and even if you spend a day out in it you cannot be sure if it falls from the sky or if it is simply some exhalation of the tired earth.

True rain hardly ever falls here. The Andes block all the moisture-laden air that comes from the Amazon basin, while the cold Humboldt Current, moving up from Antarctica, makes the sea cooler than the land and takes the humidity away from the ocean breezes. Further north, the Humboldt Current turns towards the Galápagos Islands, the sea becomes warmer than the land, and rain falls again. The desert yields to intense tropical vegetation. But by then we have reached Ecuador and Peru is left behind.

At dusk we came to the outskirts of Lima. It was called the City of the Kings in its early days, because it was founded on the feast-day of the Magi. Now it's home to nearly a third of all Peruvians. Perhaps more than a third. Over the last fifty years the population has grown from 400,000 to over 6 million and the city has almost nowhere left to go. It climbs up into the dying spurs of the Andes and sinks into gorges and ravines, where new corrugated iron roofs cluster among the rubbish of decades. It brings to mind Camus' description of Oran in *La Peste*: 'Cette ville sans pittoresque, sans végétation et sans âme . . .'

At first there's only the grey Pacific on one side and the empty desert on the other. Then, two men, solitary in the twilight, slowly making their way to the top of an immense sand dune. And, suddenly, people everywhere. They tap on the windows whenever the bus slows to avoid a child, a push-cart, or a hole in the ground. They walk or run beside us, parting smoothly ahead, like waves before an advancing ship. Piles of old, indeterminate things smoulder by the roadside, sometimes flaring up to light a face or the entrance to an alleyway. You think of one of history's great armies, encamped by night before a battle. From here on you begin to fear the moment of your arrival, when you will have to set foot among these darkened streets and half-built houses.

But the desolation of the shanty towns is more than visual. It's about an absence: the lack of almost all the familiar ways by which urban animals give shape to their lives. This is like the horrifying fascination of certain scientific experiments, where the subjects are gradually deprived of everything that makes them what they are; until in the end the observer arrives at the victorious proof that nothing is essential, only the idea of life triumphant and the absolute will to survive.

When I was last in Lima, in July 1985, Alan García was Peru's great hope. There was a military parade to celebrate his inauguration as President. It was the first time since 1912 that one elected government had lasted long enough to hand over power to another. The parade passed all the way down the Avenida Brasil, a long, treeless avenue that runs from the Plaza Bolognesi in Central Lima, straight and monotonous, until it falls into the ocean in Magdalena del Mar.

There were tanks churning up the already broken tarmac and a single Exocet missile that was cheered wherever it went. Then, surrounded by mounted soldiers, the President himself, young, *cara de niño*, a breast of medals and ribbons, glowing with plump expectation. It was a happy, messy parade, with just a minimum of order, and it might have been a warning. But not even the most cynical there could have guessed how badly things would turn out just a few years later.

Lima shares the fate of many large cities in the struggling world, but in terms of its physical decline, it is a place apart. Other Latin American cities have kept something of their past alive: Quito in Ecuador, Havana in Cuba, Cartagena in Colombia. But Lima's dazzling history leaves no trace, as if the present were too awful to cope with the memory of a time when things were better.

For over 200 years Lima ruled Spanish South America, from Panama to Tierra del Fuego. The city had the first, and for a long time, the only university on the continent. During the Enlightenment the writings of Voltaire, Rousseau, and Diderot made their way here, under the erratic eyes of the Inquisition, in the false bottoms of French wine casks. Lima was cultured, proud, and open.

It was also fabulously rich and flaunted its wealth to the world, especially during the century of absolute splendour after 1620. Symbolic of that age was the ceremonial entry of the Viceroy Duke of La Palata into Lima in 1682, when the city's merchants had two streets paved with solid silver ingots, and the Viceroy rode by on a horse whose mane was strung with pearls and whose shoes were of gold.

Lima, decadent Lima 'with the scent of women and fruit', city of flowers, of jasmine and orange blossom, and young women glimpsed through latticed windows – you'd need a great deal of imagination to bring it back to life now. Today it seems the perfect capital for what the poet García Lorca called 'this land of metal and of melancholy'. Very early in the twentieth century, long before the city was haunted by its shanty towns or strangled by the motor car, the word 'incoherence' first appears in a description of Lima. And it is this incoherence – of a city lost to itself and its past – that stays longest in the memory.

Jane is an immensely sociable woman. Even when we were children, she was quietly filling an address book from Alcock to Zamir at a time when the rest of us could have written the details of all the people we knew on the back of an envelope. Then later, when she had a house of her own, it was always full of people, even when she wasn't there; people who had nothing in common, except that once, somewhere on her travels, Jane had invited them to stay. They would come for long weekends and never leave, but nobody was ever turned away. When there was no space left indoors, newcomers slept in a truck that was parked outside on the street or in a tent that filled up most of the tiny back garden. So I wasn't surprised when she turned up some friends in Miraflores.

Miraflores is a suburb of Lima, only half an hour away from

the centre of the city down the Avenida Arequipa. It's like an urban village in the USA or the South of France. It's full of money and fashionable shops that sell nothing in particular and always seem to be empty. Some *limeños* hate Miraflores, but many would give anything to be able to live there. It doesn't have the Greenwich Village style of Barranco further down the coast; it's just new, rich and a little ordinary.

Jane's friends had sounded daunting on paper with long names cemented by *von* and *de*. But they turned out to be good company and true Peruvians. 'Of course, if we weren't', said Gustavo von Hauptman, 'we'd all be drinking in Miami by now.' He smiled, said it again, but in English this time, perfect and meticulous.

We were sitting a few yards from the Pacific, in a café on the Avenida Larco. Across the road were the remains of a bank. At six o'clock that morning there had been the proverbial small earthquake. But it was followed at eight by a large car bomb. Now the windows were boarded up. The gutters ran with powdered glass and passers-by picked their way delicately along the street, as if they were treading new snow and were uncertain where chasms lay beneath.

Well-dressed men and women fretted at nearby tables. 'The rats are pulling out. They're taking their banks and running.'

'They come. They screw you. You give it all. They go.'

'So maybe it will be better, now that we're on our own again.'

'No chance. When the foreigners start to go you know there's nothing left.'

Rumour upon rumour. Hell without end.

But none of it troubled Gustavo and his friends. They were elegant, cultured, and generous; and they wore their city with the assurance of people whose families had been there for generations and who had always had the privilege of making the rules as they went along.

Gustavo held Jane's hand in his, greeting passing friends with the other. Across the table, hidden behind owlish glasses and the smoke of a permanent cigarette, Roberto read out items from *Le*

*Monde* that intrigued him. His conversation drifted off into French, moved on through some English dialect of fifty years earlier, returned home half-heartedly to Lima. More people joined us. Waiters brought chairs and carried off empty bottles. Then suddenly, on an inside page, Roberto discovered the story of Jorge Chávez. 'Our only hero,' he said and laughed.

This was the 100th anniversary of the birth of Jorge Chávez. He had been a young and handsome Peruvian. In 1910 he became the first man in history to fly over the Alps. As he was about to land in Italy the wings of his plane fell away, and he died four days later of his injuries, with the words 'higher, ever higher' on his lips. Roberto remembered a song about him:

*Solito y en su aeroplano*
*los Alpes atravesó*
*y al universo asombró*
*el valor de este peruano.*

'It was a song the peasants in the mountains used to sing,' he said. 'Years before they had ever seen an aeroplane.'

Brecht was right about heroes. It's an unhappy land that honours Jorge Chávez. Though he was born a Peruvian he never set foot in his native land. He was the complete European. But he is remembered everywhere in Peru and Lima's international airport, a little strangely, carries his name.

By now even the waiters were unsteady on the Avenida Larco. Someone from the next table stood up and began to recite a drunken poem. A romantic, brooding piece, as far as I could tell above the noise of the traffic. As it reached what might have been its climax, Gustavo waved in Jane's direction. 'You don't like it?' he asked, as she raised her eyebrows and shrugged her shoulders. 'It's too sentimental? But look, what is there for us except suffering and death? Without public emotion there is only private misery. It's like the English,' he said, running his fingers absent-mindedly through Jane's hair. 'I know the English. They brought me up. They're like those giant fish. When they're wounded they go down very deep to die in the ocean where no one can see them.'

As eleven o'clock approached, the crowds began to thin. For a long time Lima had been under a nightly curfew. A few persistent revellers had been shot dead over the months and people now took no risks. Even the street vendors would go home early and those with nowhere to sleep would dig themselves away in quiet, unseen corners. The wealthy gave all-night parties. Invitations were marked 'de toque a toque' ('curfew to curfew'), so you knew you'd have to stay until curfew was lifted the following morning at 5 a.m.

Gustavo walked with us to the head of the Avenida Arequipa where a last cruising taxi picked us up and took us back into Central Lima. As we turned into the Avenida Tacna half an hour later, the streets were already deserted. The sky flashed yellow and blue and there was the sound of gunfire, but from far away. We reached our hotel and climbed up to our room on the seventh floor, from which, if there was anything to see, there would be a fine view. But there was nothing below us except delapidated buildings, their flat roofs covered with oil cans and rubble. The fog of the Pacific entwines itself around the polluted air of Lima's industrial zone. The orange city looks like a scene from a London winter of long ago. But the atmosphere is close and heavy, warm as a summer's evening.

With the curfew, Lima became a secret place. Troops came out on to the streets. From time to time there was the deep rumbling and flip-flop of moving tanks, followed by a silence that was total. A silence more of the country than the city, but without even a stray dog or a passing owl. Then the tanks would return and the hotel quiver, lights passed across the room from wall to wall, and your ears strained to catch the meaning of sounds you never heard in daylight.


The Lima Aguirre knew was nothing we should call a city. It was the typical Spanish-American chessboard, thirteen blocks long and nine blocks wide: 117 square islands. Straight streets, each forty feet wide, intersecting at right angles, a pattern of urban development as old as the Greek colonies of the Mediter-

38

ranean. There were probably no more than 2,000 Spaniards in the whole of Peru when Aguirre first came here in the mid-1530s. Lima then was intimate and remote.

In its early days the city sheltered dozens of market gardens, many of which survived into the late nineteenth century. As late as the 1940s Lima was still called the 'Garden City', a title that now seems cruelly unlikely. Aguirre's Lima was bordered by common land and the river Rímac: it was not until the early 1800s that the city began to reach out towards the sea. In Aguirre's time most of the white people lived around the main square, the Plaza de Armas. Black people and a few poor whites lived across the river, on the right bank of the Rímac. The Indians lived where they could, until, in 1568, a new *barrio* was created to protect them from the assaults of runaway slaves and marauding Spaniards.

Lope de Aguirre would have come to Peru by sea from the Panamanian Isthmus. There was no other way. Because of the prevailing winds he would no doubt have arrived in January or February, since it was difficult, and sometimes impossible, to reach Peru at other times of the year. If the traveller was in luck, the journey from Panama to Peru's northern border would take about ten days, but it could just as easily last three or four months. Often a ship would drop its passengers at Paita, to the north, near the modern frontier with Ecuador. The ship would then make its slow way south towards Lima's port of Callao, taking the merchandise and the heavy luggage, while its passengers made a swifter approach across the desert.

Almost all the information about Aguirre's time in Peru before he left for El Dorado comes from the chronicle of Francisco Vázquez. Nothing Vázquez says can be taken wholly on trust. He was writing to save his life and paints the darkest pictures. But much of the detail, if not the opinion, is probably not far from the truth.

Vázquez says that Aguirre worked in Peru as a horse-breaker; that he was involved in most of the revolts and disturbances that occurred in Peru in his time; and that he took part in the *entrada* of Diego de Rojas, an expedition into northern Argentina in the 1540s. He seems to have missed the battle of Chupas in September 1542, the greatest battle of the entire civil war period in which the royal governor Vaca de Castro defeated the rebellious Diego de Almagro. Vázquez claims that Aguirre 'hid himself' in the nearby town of Huamanga, in order to avoid the fighting, but there is no certainty that he was even in Peru at the time.

Aguirre also missed the rebellion of Francisco Pizarro's youngest brother, Gonzalo, which occupied Peru from 1544 until 1548. Aguirre, according to Vázquez, 'remained in Nicaragua' during these years, returning only after the defeat of Gonzalo and his subsequent execution at the hands of the royal emissary Pedro de la Gasca. There is no doubt, however, that Aguirre fought on the royalist side against the last of Peru's great rebels, Francisco Hernández Girón. Both Vázquez and Aguirre himself tell us that he was wounded in the leg at the battle of Chuquinca and that the wound left him permanently lame.

At Chuquinca he fought under Alonso de Alvarado, who has been called 'one of the most presumptuous men in Peru' and who, according to Garcilaso, was plunged into such deep melancholy by his defeat in battle that 'he never after enjoyed a day of pleasure or contentment, but gradually dwindled away until he died'. Hernández Girón, who was, in his way, as presumptuous as his opponent – his wife was called 'Queen of Peru' for a time – was finally defeated in October 1554, bringing to an end a period of more than fifteen years of almost continual strife among the Spanish of Peru.


There are times when the excitement of travel fades before a much older emotion: the quest for order. Jane and I spent weeks in Lima, subtly reinforcing in each other an unwillingness to leave. Lima was, no doubt, a bad place to be. An American news magazine had declared that it was the fourth worst city in the world, a finding that amused some *limeños* and surprised others who thought they had already touched the bottom. Two guerrilla groups were fighting for control of the capital and the streets were patrolled by young, unhappy conscripts. But in reality we saw little. Each morning we would go out and buy the newspapers to find out what was happening a few streets or a few hundred miles away. Our lives became more and more hemmed in by small, day-to-day problems: it was the shortage of batteries for our radio that troubled me most often, the failings of the postal service that worried Jane.

On our last evening in Lima we walked back to our hotel from a friend's apartment on the Avenida Abancay. The city had become overwhelmingly familiar. We passed the Sheraton, with more flags than guests, and the US Embassy, fortified and silent. Sometimes you saw dark wooden balconies, worm-eaten and ragged, once part of an architectural tradition that flowed from the Near East, via North Africa, Andalusia, the Canary Islands, San Juan, Havana, and Cartagena, to finish up here on the edge of the Pacific.

All cities have their smell, but I can never remember the smell of Lima. Nor its colour, since it seems to live without colour. It takes so much from the sky which, for months on end, is always the same. In other countries where the weather never changes you discover variations after a while. Here, under the fog, there are none; or else they're too familiar, like countless winter days at home.

On street corners and patches of waste ground people stand about and wait. I've never seen a city where so many had so little to do. But a woman from the US said to me: 'If people believe capitalism doesn't work, they should come to Lima and see for themselves.' And it's true. There's a competitive market here of extraordinary purity. You can buy anything from the street vendors. They come from distant shanty towns, often spending five or six hours a day on Lima's old buses. They sell cigarettes in twos and threes, airmail envelopes, tables of chemical elements, and charts of human anatomy.

I once watched a man trying to sell an enormous spanner. It was useless, except for industrial purposes, but he went in and out of every restaurant on the Jirón de la Unión until someone took it from him. He was a small man and when he reappeared without his spanner he was almost indistinguishable in the crowd. Only a tiny mark of satisfaction, or maybe revenge, told you this had been a successful day.

Now, as we turned a corner, a young boy came down the street on a kind of skateboard. But he had no legs. Around his neck he wore a dirty pencilled sign in poor Spanish: 'I'm hungry. Please help me.' Shoppers moved to let him pass, but absent-mindedly and without interest. Forty per cent of Peru's population is under the age of fourteen.

Nobody notices the passions of this city either, though they are clothed in almost as many variations as its destitution. Since economics determine that love must be public, decency requires that no one should look. The cool displays of northern European lovers have no counterpart here. Wherever you go there are couples on benches or under wizened bushes, slipping gradually more horizontal as the darkness of evening colours the fog around them.

'Perhaps it's the opposite of what you think,' Jane said. 'With all those barriers, all those inhibitions. Perhaps it's really the best place in the world to be in love. Only what do they do in summer when the fog has gone? Just think, all those couples, all praying for another winter like this.'

We reached our hotel through a fog that had deepened so that we almost lost our way. The fruit-seller who lived most of his life on the pavement opposite was packing up his stall. There was a family funeral, he said. His stall was the only colourful place in the district. Jane bought some *chirimoyas* for the next day, the fruit that is called 'custard apple' in English, though some used to call it 'sweetsop' or 'bullock's heart'. It has a thick green scaly rind. 'Foreigners don't often buy from me,' said the seller. 'One of them told me the fruit carries diseases in its skin that you cannot see.'

The next morning we left Lima and took a bus north along the Pan-American highway. It was a good bus, comfortable – a rarity. It's not so much the fault of the buses as the roads they have to travel on. An opinion poll in 1987 asking what people thought of members of the government found that only 6 per cent approved of the Minister of Transport, a scale of disaster equalled only by the Minister of Fisheries.

The bus passes through miles of shanty towns. Then there is only desert. Sometimes you see the Pacific below, as the highway rises steeply beyond the Lima plain. Grey waves break far out to sea, almost beyond the point of visibility. Sand blows constantly across the road and bulldozers work to keep it open. When the Incas built their roads through the desert, they placed wooden stakes at intervals, as a guide to travellers. This called for organisation in the largely timberless land of coastal Peru. But the Spanish, either because they did not understand or were in too much of a hurry, took the stakes away and used them for firewood.

There are a few small towns on the road, some poor and unkempt, some set in green valleys, where irrigation turns the desert into Lima's market garden.

At Paramonga there is an old adobe fortress. Even at the time of the Conquest it was in ruins, and, as the chronicler Cieza de León said, 'now . . . it has no function, save to bear witness to what once it was.' To the south there's a turning to the east and the long road into the Andes begins. Soon the air changes; the tropical sun shines through the fog and now the desert starts to look the way a desert should. The sand is golden and covered with large boulders. The road follows the Río de la Fortaleza (River of the Fortress) and there's a narrow strip of vegetation that dies abruptly where it strays too far from the water. This is the Cordillera Negra, the black mountains on which no moisture ever falls.

Then the air sharpens again as you climb higher and you enter a region that is green and forested, sometimes called the Switzerland of Peru. The road turns endlessly upon itself, apparently making no forward progress until, suddenly, you are able to see the white mountains of the Cordillera Blanca far away.

In the early evening we reached the town of Huarás. Friends

43

who saw it many years ago have told me it was once an attractive place. But it has suffered terribly from its position. It was buried in a famous avalanche in December 1941 and then again in 1958. In 1970 an earthquake destroyed it almost entirely. It's been rebuilt and has nothing special left; it's an ordinary town surrounded by some of the most beautiful mountains in the world.

A few miles outside Huarás, at Baños de Monterrey, is my favourite hotel in Peru. It's cheap and has only a dozen rooms. But everything else is very grand. The dining room is permanently laid out as if a hundred guests were expected at any minute and the grounds swarm with colour and scent, like a tropicalised English country house. There are flowers everywhere; in bedrooms and passageways, in tiny unseen corners. They spread out on to the terrace, at first neat and disciplined, then chaotic as the land falls slowly down to a noisy stream.

Hot springs, red with iron, bubble out of the earth and collect in a pool where you can swim in the cold of early morning or the heat of midday. It's a hotel where people used to come to relax after walking in the mountains.

Baños de Monterrey has always been a refuge. For us it felt safe and far from Peru and we settled in to enjoy it.

# THREE

'HAVE YOU SEEN the tortoises of Arequipa?' The hotel manager looked at Jane across oceans of paperwork. She looked at me, suspiciously. She thinks the word *tortuga* must mean something besides 'tortoise'. But the manager intercepts, for he's an intelligent man. He makes a crab-like gesture over his desk. So he does mean tortoise.

Arequipa is a desert city far to the south of Peru, towards the border with Chile, where the novelist Mario Vargas Llosa was born. It has a perfect climate: they say the sun shines 360 days a year. But I'd never heard of its tortoises. The manager was about to explain when the phone rang. It was only months later that someone told us Arequipa is a centre for tortoise-racing; and that still didn't help until someone else explained that the point of these races is to parody the speed of Peruvian bureaucracy.

We sat by the side of the pool in the late afternoon sun. The manager invited himself to join us, tactfully, without insisting. In your place, he says, I would return to Lima. Jane gave him a cool look, which he correctly interpreted and followed up with a solution: if we wanted to go on, we could walk from here to Chavín de Huántar, four days away. From there we would find a bus or a truck to take us to the town of Llamellín, where we could buy supplies. After which, he wasn't sure, but by following what the Spanish call a *camino de herradura* ('horseshoe path') it might be possible to reach Huacrachuco after five or six more days' walking. By then, he said gravely, you would not be so far

45

from the Inca highway you are looking for.

The only problem, he went on, was that between Llamellín and Huacrachuco there might be no villages. So there would be no food. But this, he concluded, with a triumph of sudden reversal, might be the great advantage. For, he concluded, where there were no friendly faces, perhaps there would be no hostile ones either.

The mountain path to Chavín de Huántar begins by the Puente Bedoya, a bridge near nowhere in particular, a few miles outside Huarás. The hotel manager walked with us to the bus that would take us there, shook our hands, and wished us luck.

Rural buses in Peru, as in so many places where resources are scarce, don't leave at a fixed time. They wait until they're full. First the seats fill up, then people stand, then more people push in and the space constantly readjusts, each new wave accommodated, silently and without protest. The exterior begins to fill up, too. Odd things appear on the roof, baskets and parcels and animals in sacks. Finally the vehicle reaches a point of explosive balance, where no one can get on or off, and from then on you just wait. The street sellers open up tiny spaces in the crowd, and woollen caps, packets of biscuits, fresh bread, and dripping ice creams pass into the bus, from which, by some process, money is extracted by return. Eventually, for no apparent reason, a driver appears and off you go.

At the Puente Bedoya we got down and sat for a while by the side of the road, listening to the rattle of the bus as it twisted and turned onwards to the horizon. Five minutes later you could still hear the faint, exhausted sound as it slowed below walking pace and struggled to complete another ascent. Then there was silence and we stretched out on the ground, revelling in the sense of recovered space.

Four hundred years ago whole armies moved through the mountains faster than we can now. The chroniclers complained, of course, that the roads were constantly deteriorating; while on

46

the edge of the jungle, where Ursúa's expedition was gathering, the roads had never been good, for the area lay beyond the limits of the old Inca empire. But Ursúa seems to have come and gone as he wished, like some travelling salesman or presidential candidate. He rode a horse where the country was suitable and enjoyed the dubious luxury of a travelling hammock elsewhere.

His main concerns in the early days were the obvious ones: he needed men, food, equipment, guns, ships, and horses. None of these was cheap, except the men; some of them were extravagantly expensive. The responsibility for obtaining supplies traditionally fell on the leader of the expedition. He usually bought on credit from local merchants and then resold to members of the expedition, also on credit. This meant that indebtedness was a fact of life for all, and that an expedition which did not promise rapid returns was going to be a vulnerable one.

Ursúa was not completely ignorant of what lay ahead. By the 1550s the Spanish already knew something about jungle travel; and they also knew that the Amazon was a very long river indeed. They were not sure exactly where it rose, but they had learnt that it ended in the Atlantic Ocean, or, as they called it then, the North Sea. This they knew from a great expedition under Gonzalo Pizarro which had left Quito in search of El Dorado in February 1541. Gonzalo had taken 220 Spaniards with him, 4,000 Indians, 200 horses, 2,000 live hogs with almost as many dogs, and a contingent of llamas.

They went down the river Napo and, at a certain point, Gonzalo halted the main expedition and sent a detachment of about sixty men under the command of Francisco de Orellana to forage for supplies. Orellana and his men never rejoined the main group. They kept on down the Napo, entering the Amazon a year after leaving Quito. They then continued downriver and reached the Atlantic Ocean in August 1542. From there they travelled up the east coast of South America and, in September, arrived on the island of Cubagua, off the mainland of Venezuela; after which most of the survivors returned to Peru to

47

fight on the royalist side in the civil war, against Gonzalo Pizarro, their former commander.

With Orellana on his descent of the Amazon was the Dominican friar, Gaspar de Carvajal, who subsequently wrote an account of the affair. It is the brilliantly understated story of a born survivor. Carvajal lost an eye in an Indian attack on the Amazon and came close to death, but he went on to found the first Dominican monastery in Peru and lived on in Lima to the age of eighty. Carvajal's chronicle should have left nobody in any doubt that the jungle was a miserable place to travel. Supplies had quickly been exhausted. They were forced to eat a hundred of their horses and a thousand of their dogs, but still men went hungry and died of starvation, as well as fatigue and disease.

Orellana and his party were reduced to eating hides, straps of leather, and the soles of their shoes cooked with herbs. Some searched out roots in the forest, but, not knowing which were edible, poisoned themselves. Indian tribes harassed them at various times, not least in the lower reaches of the river, where Orellana encountered the famous women warriors whom they called Amazons, after the legendary women from beyond the frontiers of the ancient Greek world.

Carvajal was in Lima when Ursúa was organizing his own expedition. They must have known each other and must have spoken about the prospects of another journey down the Amazon. Carvajal could have said there was no gold or silver on the river. Perhaps he did. But the chronicler Ortiguera suggests that people only took from his story what they wanted to hear: 'These things', he says, 'so strangely moved the hearts and minds of men to see them with their own eyes . . . that it was impossible to believe.'

So Ursúa went on with the business of raising men, money, and supplies. In Topesana his chosen men under Juan Corvo were building ships. They eventually finished eleven in all. Most were huge barges, each capable of carrying thirty to forty horses, as well as men and provisions. Several of the chroniclers likened these barges to the 'barcas de Córdoba' which they must have seen transporting goods on the Guadalquivir between Córdoba and Seville. They also built two ships which the chroniclers call *bergantines*. The 'brigantine' at that date was very different from the two-masted, square-rigged vessel of later times. It was a small ship, much used in the Mediterranean in the fourteenth and fifteenth centuries. It was equipped for both sailing and rowing, and it was fast and easily manoeuvrable – the ideal ship for pirates, hence its name, which derives from the Italian word for 'brigand'.

Orellana and his party had also taken two brigantines on their descent of the Amazon and both ships had survived the journey to Cubagua. The fate of Ursúa's vessels was, characteristically, to be quite different.

Much has been written about the weapons which the Spanish brought to the New World and which, inevitably, loomed large in the preparations for any expedition. Ursúa, like Orellana, relied on two main aggressive weapons: the crossbow and the harquebus.

The crossbow had been in use in Europe for centuries. It was a weapon much admired by Richard the Lionheart, who was to die from a crossbow bolt at the siege of Le Mans in 1199. By the time of the Spanish conquest of Peru the crossbow was fast approaching the end of its useful life on the battlefield, but it could still be a devastating weapon in trained hands.

The harquebus lay at the other extreme of technology. It was the latest and the best that Europe could offer, the immediate predecessor of the musket. How good the harquebus was in practice remains the subject of an interesting controversy – how it compared in terms of accuracy and rate of fire with the crossbow or the longbow, for example. Its range is variously estimated at between 250 and 600 feet, as against the crossbow's maximum of 130 feet.

One thing, however, is certain. From the time that hand guns first appeared in Europe in the fourteenth century, standards had been gradually improving; and, by the early years of the sixteenth century, it was the harquebus that had enabled the Spanish armies to transform military science and to lay the basis for modern military fire action.

The harquebus was invented in Spain in the mid-fifteenth century. The weapon which the *conquistadores* brought to Peru in the 1530s had been battle-tested in the Italian wars and had undergone numerous changes. Nevertheless, it was still a weapon best suited to the battlefield, rather than to general use. It depended for ignition on a smouldering slow match, so it was of no use in an emergency. Gunpowder at this time was poor in quality and slow to burn. Damp weather brought immediate problems and heavy rain put the harquebus out of action altogether. It was certainly not a weapon designed for the climate of the Amazon basin, though its psychological effect on native peoples who had never known the noise and smell of guns was immense.

The other great psychological weapon in the hands of the Spanish was the horse. Garcilaso, who was the son of a Spanish *conquistador* and an Inca princess, writes:

> Until the coming of the Spaniards, the Indians were so simple that the sight of anything that they had never beheld before was enough to cause them to bow down and recognize the inventor as a divine child of the Sun. Thus nothing impressed them so much, causing them to regard the Spaniards as gods and surrender to them at the beginning of the Conquest, as the sight of them fighting on such fierce animals as horses appeared to them, and able to shoot with harquebuses and kill men at a distance of two or three hundred paces. Because of these two things especially . . . the Indians thought the Spaniards were children of the Sun and gave in to them with little resistance.

Even so, it seems strange to us now that Ursúa should have spent much of his energy trying to raise horses for the expedition. Horses are powerful animals on flat or rolling ground, but they are poorly suited to the mountains and it is hard to see what function they could have had on a river like the Amazon.

In the early days after the Conquest, horses were beyond price in Peru. Garcilaso says that on the rare occasions when one was offered for sale it might fetch 4-6,000 *pesos*, while the leader of the royalist forces before the battle of Chuquinca offered 10,000 *pesos* for a horse and its attendant. Later on, supply and demand were reconciled and, by the end of the sixteenth century, the price had fallen to 3-400 *pesos*. At the time of Ursúa's adventure into the Amazon, a large number of horses still represented an extravagant investment none the less.

There are only two explanations for Ursúa's insistence. One was prestige. In the sixteenth century a horse was the most important status-symbol in Spanish society, as it had been throughout the Middle Ages. You couldn't take yourself seriously if you didn't own a horse. And then Ursúa must have believed a little in his own propaganda: his expedition would find good land to settle and, when it did, it was inconceivable to a Spaniard of his class that a horse would not be essential to the good life.

The chroniclers differ widely as to how many weapons and horses Ursúa finally brought to Santa Cruz de Saposoa. There were certainly not fewer than 150 horses and there may have been twice that number. They were almost never to be heard of again, except as food for the starving. But of the forty cross-bows and the hundred or so harquebuses we shall continue to hear a good deal.


We left the Puente Bedoya. We passed a group of people gazing intensely at the ground. A child came up to us with large, mournful eyes. 'It's dead,' he said. A cow lay stretched out, a dark mass on the road. It might have been asleep. It didn't look injured. The child raised his eyes to the high cliffs which bordered the road and said: 'It fell.'

We began to climb a path towards the village of Olleros. The country was dry and motionless in the heat of the afternoon. Eucalyptus trees spread all across the hillside, Spain's great gift to the landscape of Peru, green and shady among the indigenous yellows and browns. Olleros was quiet, almost empty, the houses dark, windowless, with dirt floors.

We met a man in a smart suit carrying a briefcase. He could

have been on his way to work in any of the world's capital cities. He looked us over, unable to decide his response. Then, acknowledging that he was no less out of place here than we were, he said, 'I've come on business'.

He said it as if nothing except business would ever bring anyone to the village. But that only excited his curiosity, since it was obvious we must have come for something else.

'We're walking to Chavín,' said Jane helpfully, to fill a silence.

'Chavín de Huántar?' he asked, as if there was more than one. 'You're walking to Chavín de Huántar?' Suddenly he allowed himself a glance of pure condescension. Then, finally assured of his superiority, he became quite friendly and talkative. 'But it will take you a week to get there. If you do get there. You will freeze to the ground every night. There is nothing to eat. There are bad people.'

'Have you ever done it?' Jane asked him, half playful, half malicious.

'I am not a flock of sheep,' he replied, setting the record straight. 'This is the twentieth century.'

'But people come from all over the world to walk to Chavín.'

'Then the world must have more time to waste than I do. At least', he said, lowering his mouth towards Jane's ear, 'you should take a guide. But whatever you do, don't camp near here. They will cut off your head.'

We passed on through Olleros. There was a small library in the square with a scruffy reading room. Outside it, the dead cow was now being cut up. Two men working over the carcass waved to us to come and see. But at that moment a young woman and a girl appeared. 'Do you have medicines?' they asked.

'What's the matter?'

'I have a pain all over my body,' said the woman. The girl, too, said she was in pain. 'It hurts in my back and my legs and my head. My eyes are bad.' I looked into the girl's eyes. They were misty and unfocused.

I recalled a time seven years before, when I had travelled with a Cuban doctor through the small villages on the eastern coast of Nicaragua. Places that were later to be caught up in the civil war, but which were very quiet then. The hottest, quietest places you could imagine. Villages with names like Pearl Lagoon and Kukra Hill, where they spoke English with the accent of the Caribbean or South London, so that it didn't feel strange to be there.

Late one afternoon we came to a tiny settlement on the bank of a river. At once people descended complaining of pain in every part of their body. They all wanted medicine. Young children peered into the doctor's bag as if Santa Claus had just arrived with gifts and happiness for everyone. The older people pushed and pleaded. 'In the old days', the doctor said, 'they used to hand out pills to bring in the votes at election time. It's not medicine you need to cure most of the sickness here.'

I'd often thought of that lesson since. But now there were only two of us, with our malaria pills and vitamins, and two of them, undernourished and expectant. Jane gave them some aspirin and they went off slowly along a narrow path between two rows of houses.

We walked past a small church, long disused. It had a square tower and a tiled roof. There was a faded white cross on a blue door and a brown stain edging down the whitewashed walls. Then we left the last of the houses and climbed into open country. Immense clouds were piled high up into the blue sky. There were a few low trees close by and, further away, dark, treeless hills already looking cold in the late afternoon light. After a time we seemed to be utterly alone. But in the Andes people often live in isolation, rather than in communities. We noted a small house with a snow-capped peak rising far behind it, like an invitation to a holiday in the Alps. Five children ran out over the dry grass to see us and a well-fed dog cantered along behind them. The children wore warm clothes and the land was neat and cared for, partitioned by dry-stone walls.

The day was fading quickly towards a winter night and we pitched our tent. By the time I came back from a nearby stream with water, it was dark. We cooked a camping meal of sugar and starch and went to bed.

The country is always full of noises and it takes time to make peace with them in the darkness. We lay awake and tried to sort out sounds that might have been animals or birds or something unknown. Then I fell asleep. I had slept badly for a few hours when I felt Jane's hand on my sleeping bag trying to wake me.

'Someone's moving around outside.'

'Are you sure?'

'Well, with luck perhaps it's a ghost,' she said, though I knew she was serious.

We unzipped the tent flap and looked out. There was only darkness. Then a light through the trees. Then another, and more, and they began to move, though whether towards us or away was hard to tell. We'd brought our packs into the tent to shelter them from the heavy dew, so it took time to get past them and out into the open air. By then the lights had come much closer. They were swaying rapidly up and down and now there was a noise, of chanting or lamentation.

The grass was frozen under our bare feet and the southern sky was bright with thousands of unfamiliar stars. The wind blew softly behind us, carrying all detail of the sound away. A procession passed by, twenty or thirty lights flickering and dying among the trees. Then there was nothing and we were alone. The silence was like an open wound and our minds explored each nerve in turn to decide on what was real and what was not.

The next morning the countryside was deserted and empty of all signs. We climbed on into a broad valley. The land was strewn with giant boulders, the debris of glacial streams. The path became a mass of tiny stones, but walking was easy here. This route led across the only low pass for miles around and it's still well trodden. A young girl of about twelve passed by, at twice our speed, on her way to pick up a flock of goats. A single woman, veiled in black and driving a donkey, crossed in the other direction.

As we climbed over a slight rise, we spotted a flock of sheep coming towards us, looking flustered on seeing their path blocked. Behind them was a woman on a mule, with a child walking at her side. Mother and child wore brown felt hats, the child's so broad you couldn't tell if it covered a boy or a girl. As we came closer, we saw the woman was breast-feeting a baby. She turned the mule sideways on as she greeted us and the wind from the mountains suddenly caught them in the face and the baby began to cry. We told her of our adventure in the night. She looked concerned and a little excited.

'There are men who go out after dark and when they find a traveller they cut his throat and open his stomach and take out the insides.' Jane was sceptical about this, but keen to hear more.

'They take out the fat and they make things with it, things to cure you when you are sick.'

'Have you ever seen these people?'

'How can you ever be sure? They carry a large knife and they wear their hair long. Sometimes they have a great coat that comes down to their knees. But don't worry,' she said, looking at me, 'they won't do you any harm.'

Now the scepticism was all mine. 'How can you be sure of that?' I asked.

'Because they are like you. They have pale skin and light hair and they look as if they haven't eaten for many days. I don't think they will dare to touch you.'

Later that day we came into high meadow land. We passed large herds of cattle grazing on the rough grasses. The wind rose all afternoon and we were on an open plain without shelter. In the twilight five hooded men rode by on horseback, with a dog at their heels. We spent a sleepless night, listening to the wind and rain on the roof of the tent. Towards dawn the rain stopped. It was quiet then and in the early light we could see that snow had fallen.

That day we crossed over the pass. The mountains below the snow line were very black in the sun; there were blue icefalls that dazzled the eyes and large stretches of rock with the colour and texture of raw coal. Small streams rushed from ledge to ledge, turning gradually into waterfalls as they fell further down. I remember glacial lakes, unruffled, like lumps of solid metal, the howling of the wind, and the path sloping upwards, hour after hour, towards a point 16,000 feet high. Everything became dull and detached. You'd observe sudden weaknesses in your muscles and sometimes a far away beating that turned out to be your heart.

We arrived in Chavín late at night, in the middle of a thunder storm. The streets were completely buried in mud and the only place to stay was a kind of ruined bungalow that smelled of sewage and long abandon. When Ronald Wright came here a few years before, he noticed a slogan on one of the walls: 'Mr Mayor, why haven't we got water or drainage?' The writing seemed to have vanished now, leaving the question, obviously, unanswered.

Chavín is a small place. A bakery, a couple of general stores, a few restaurants. More restaurants, indeed, than it would merit by its size alone. But then Chavín is also the guardian of one of the most important archaeological sites in the Americas. It was home to a culture that flourished for 800 years during the first millennium BC; and such was its prestige that a faint memory still survived when the Spanish came to Peru fifteen hundred years later.

Chavín was almost certainly a great cult centre and place of pilgrimage, with an influence that spread over a wide area of what is now Peru, along the coast and into the north and central highlands. Where the culture originated has been much discussed: it certainly wasn't at Chavín itself. Some argue that it must have developed in the Amazon basin, because its art shows animals like the monkey and the jaguar. Others, convinced that the Amazon has always been one of history's backwaters, suggest a coastal source and claim that the apparently tropical motifs have been wrongly identified.

The remains of old Chavín lie in a hot, dry valley, with the mountains on one side and the river Mosna on the other. From a large sunken courtyard, surrounded by symmetrically placed stone staircases, you climb, through several levels of terracing, to the massive temple that dominates the site. Originally this was a pyramid 230 feet square at the base, now much eroded, but still rising to between forty and fifty feet in places. To the north and south of the sunken courtyard there are two rectangular platforms, where spectators may have gathered to watch the progress of the religious ceremonies.

Whatever the origins of Chavín culture, its power was clearly based on terror. On the side of the temple that faces out towards the road, there's a single stone-carved head set into the wall. Once there were many of these heads, placed at intervals around the temple walls; some were destroyed in a landslide in 1945, the rest have been moved to safety underground.

If you pursue the heads to their new resting place in the labyrinth of interior galleries you see that they have lost none of their horror. Wherever you shine your torch, faces look out at you. They sometimes represent animals, but most are human, often grossly deformed by animal features. They have terrible fangs or they crawl with twisted snakes. They leer and scream, some tortured to the end of their resistance, some sharing dark and hideous secrets which are hidden from us, all wondrously alive.

Down one of the narrow passageways, you find yourself in the unmistakable presence of a god. He has two fangs and is crowned with snakes. His hands have long, pointed fingernails, and his right arm is raised. This is the snarling deity whose name, since 1899, has been *El Lanzón* ('The Dagger'). The statue, fifteen feet high, is a block of carved white granite that tapers towards the ground. It looks as if it has just been thrown into the earth, so that you might still expect to see it quivering. But it has occupied the same space for 3,000 years.

The interior galleries confirm the dualism of Chavín, a culture that reveals itself through opposing images of light and darkness, day and night. As the temple is orientated towards the rising sun, so the galleries keep watch over an eternal darkness; while in the iconography of Chavín, there are birds suggesting lightness and freedom, alongside serpents and cat-like creatures that speak of terror and the night.

It is the darkness that survives most tellingly.

We had been in Chavín only a few days when we realised there was no way forward from there. Fighting to the north had cut off the path towards Huacrachuco; while, to the east, an alternative route into the Amazon basin, through the valley of the Huallaga river, was also blocked. Two days before we reached Chavín, the government had placed the Upper Huallaga under a state of emergency, as the forces of Sendero Luminoso drew a net ever tighter around Peru's main coca-growing area.

Not that this was so clear from Chavín. People said nothing – no drama, no hoarse whisper in the night, like in the old films where someone obligingly comes to tell you: 'Señor, it ees dangerous, they weel keel you.' It was more like the mist on a summer's morning which gives shape and then deforms, where sometimes you see and sometimes everything is hidden.

We were about 180 miles from Saposoa and the Central Huallaga, but there was no choice, except to return to the coast and make a final detour still further to the north, through Trujillo. Ursúa himself had come this long way round at least twice, as he moved between Lima and Saposoa. But then, as we shall see, he had a distinct incentive.

We retraced our steps towards the Pacific. A series of hardships now dull and familiar. A trail that once tempted the eye to a remote and snow-covered horizon, now leading down towards the entirely known.

I was reminded of one of the most famous journeys in the history of the Conquest, which had brought Hernando Pizarro this way early in 1533, only months after the Spanish first arrived in Peru. Pizarro had seen this country as few Europeans were ever to do. He came down from Cajamarca with fourteen horsemen and nine foot-soldiers, to plunder the Inca temple at Pachacámac, just to the south of modern Lima. He marvelled at the Inca highway which brought the company through the mountains. 'Nowhere in Christendom', he wrote later, 'were ever seen such fine roads.'

They came down the Callejón de Huaylas, the alleyway formed by the Cordillera Negra to the west and'the Blanca to the east. Everywhere they were met with celebration, colour, music, and dance. They saw ordered fields of potatoes and maize and crossed over passes where their horses were almost buried in the snow. They passed through Huarás, whose lord was then an Indian called Pumacapillay, from whom they received food in abundance and servants to carry their belongings. They were amazed at the richness of the land, the many towns, the large population. In just a few months this world vanished, as the cultures of the Andes fell before the violence and everyday diseases of European life.

From Huarás we took a bus to the coast. It wandered skywards, through gradients so steep that even the donkeys along the way seemed to have given up hope. After three hours Huarás was still there, spread out below us, and only a little smaller. We crossed back over the Cordillera Negra. It was hot and dusty. The bus was unbearable with the windows closed, but when you opened them a thick orange sediment drifted in, settling over bare arms and between your teeth.

We stopped for lunch in a poor, dispiriting town, where the only restaurant seethed with flies from an outdoor toilet next to the kitchen. Jane found some chocolate in her pack that had been through cycles of melting and refreezing in the mountains and tasted of nothing. We bought some *pákay* from a fruit-seller – it is moist and white, safely lodged in a large pod, like an enormous French bean.

All around the town there were banana plantations whose trees swayed top-heavy in the light breeze. Bananas are a wonderful food; only manioc and rice can compete in the number of calories per acre. The famous explorer Alexander von Humboldt once suggested that all banana groves be abolished by decree, since they made life too easy and prevented the Indians from understanding that the meaning of existence lies, after all, in hard work and discipline.

The bus drove away. The bananas disappeared and we looked

again at the absolute desert of the Peruvian coast. Nothing but sand and stones; empty spaces of flat red land, with the occasional bush or discarded petrol can.

We reached the sea at Casma, at the mouth of the Río Sechín. The town was destroyed in 1970, in the same earthquake that levelled Huarás. From here the road turns north along the coast and, after a time, people began to close the windows at the approaches to Chimbote.

You could never guess that Chimbote was once a favourite place for honeymoon couples. It's a large city now with some of the worst social problems in Peru. Less than 20 per cent of the workforce has stable employment and three-quarters of the population live in the bleakest of shanty towns. When cholera returned to Peru in the early 1990s, it spread more easily here than anywhere else. In the 1950s Chimbote was a thriving fishing village; but the fish have gone and boats lie idle. You can smell the decay from miles around.

Only relief workers or the dedicated voyeurs of human misery would choose to stay here. So when the bus from Huarás set us down, we joined the queue for a *colectivo* to Trujillo. *Colectivos* are like taxis in most ways, but they wait until they're full before going anywhere. So a journey in one is often as crowded and as uncomfortable as a bus ride.

The *colectivo* had barely slowed to a halt when seven of us leapt in; and before it could move away a young boy with sad eyes and a poodle pulled the door handle off in his haste to join us. Both boy and poodle looked as if they'd been having a hard time in Chimbote and couldn't get out fast enough. Squashed and silent, we drove north across the desert and, in the early evening, we reached Trujillo.

Capital of northern Peru, as Arequipa is capital of the south, Trujillo was founded late in November 1534 as a way-station for travellers coming down the coast towards Lima. Its name honours the birthplace of Francisco Pizarro in Estremaduran Trujillo, 'leaving to the latter [city] the glory of calling him a son, and to the new [city] the privilege of acknowledging him as a father', as one of the early chroniclers put it. The city has its place in the story of Lope de Aguirre, but for one reason only: it was the home of doña Inés de Atienza. She is the *femme fatale* of El Dorado, 'the most beautiful woman in Peru', according to the chronicler Custodio Hernández, and the cause, according to everyone, of the downfall of her lover, Pedro de Ursúa.

At this distance there's no hope of finding out what sort of woman doña Inés really was, but there's no doubt at all that she was beautiful; no one denies that. And her particular beauty was something novel and rare in the world, for she was one of the first of the *mestizas*, the new race of women born to a Spanish father and an Indian mother. Whether she was virtuous or depraved, madonna or siren, instigator or victim, we'll never know. But she certainly left a mark on those who saw her. She excited men and they died on the Amazon for the illusion of possessing her.

She is always called *doña*, but that doesn't necessarily tell us much about her social station. The title *don* for a man signified high social rank in those days, but many women called themselves *doña*. Doña Inés was the daughter of a man from Trujillo called Blas de Atienza, whom Garcilaso mentions in passing. At some time in her life she was married to a man from Piura, but seems to have been widowed by the time Ursúa met her. Perhaps they first saw each other when he passed through Trujillo on his way to organise the base camp in Santa Cruz. Certainly he was already involved with her a few months later when he came this way a second time, for the Viceroy himself had to intervene, ordering him to delay no longer in the city on her account.

Trujillo was a small place then. Ursúa was young and handsome. Doña Inés was beautiful and free. It takes little imagination to guess the sequence of events. And none of it would have mattered, if Ursúa hadn't been the leader of an expedition and if doña Inés hadn't insisted on going with him.

In principle, there was nothing much wrong about a woman

going off on a journey with her lover. If she was a married woman, then she had to stay at home. But if she wasn't, she had considerable freedom. James Lockhart mentions the case of a man who took his lover into the wilds of northern Argentina on the *entrada* of Diego de Rojas. The couple lived there for years together and finally married.

But with Ursúa it was different. The fact that he was a leader, responsible for the good conduct of an expedition, made it foolhardy for him to have a lover. Whether doña Inés was just 'a beautiful girl', as Garcilaso says, or whether, as Vázquez suggests, she used witchcraft to ensnare her man, the point which all the chroniclers make is that she should never have been there at all. The presence of doña Inés, says Vázquez, led Ursúa to neglect his duties and this 'was the main reason for the death of the Governor and our own total destruction'.

There is not much more we can say about doña Inés on the evidence we have. But three hundred years after the events, a passionate Victorian named Clements Markham fell in love with her. Markham wrote an introduction to an English translation of one of the Ursúa chronicles and he took it on himself to defend Inés against all criticism. If one of her detractors tried to blacken her reputation by insinuating she had lesbian tendencies, as well as a considerable appetite for men, Markham saw her as the personification of his ideal woman:

> Inés . . . a young, beautiful, and spirited woman . . . gave [Ursúa] her heart; but hers was no common love; it is not every woman, gently nurtured and accustomed to the comforts of civilised life, who would have willingly encountered the appalling hardships of a search for El Dorado, and a voyage down a great river . . .

He even has an answer for those who criticise her for taking another lover after Ursúa was dead:

> If she was guilty of any fault, after the death of Ursúa . . . which I do not believe, let it be remembered that the poor broken-hearted girl was utterly helpless, and in the hands

62

of incarnate fiends, with hearts harder than the nether mill stone.

Clements Markham is still remembered in Peru, though not always with affection. As a young employee of the British India Office in the 1850s, he travelled in South America. He smuggled Cinchona plants out of Peru and carried them back to India, where he was much celebrated, for the Cinchona is a major source of quinine.

Modern Trujillo is big, with the energy of a wealthy city, and, after Lima, it felt very sane. We lived for several weeks on the northern outskirts in a fantasy hotel, modelled on a Bavarian castle, its upper floor protected by turrets and battlements. There was a fine view from there, across the city to the desert beyond. At night it was extravagantly lit in wild reds and greens, with tropical plants so aggressive, so invasive, you could never think of them as real.

Trujillo is the home of *aprismo* and of its founder, Víctor Raúl Haya de la Torre. The APRA is Peru's oldest political party. In its sixty years it has moved across the entire ideological spectrum. Revolutionary and repressed in the 1930s, then violently anti-communist in the 1940s and '50s. Recently it's settled down in the middle, as a moderate social democratic party; and, as such, it was finally permitted to take power. After years of disaster and humiliation it won the elections of 1985 and its new leader Alan García moved into the Presidential Palace.

In pre-Inca times, the area around Trujillo saw the development of two remarkable civilisations: Moche, which dates from the early years of the Christian era, and Chimú, a culture which expanded rapidly after AD 1200 and fell around 1470 before a surge of Inca power from the south.

Moche is famous above all for its red and white pottery. It is so beautifully drawn that it gives a feeling of intimacy we shall never find again in the pre-Hispanic art of Peru. It showed men fighting, hunting, fishing, or dancing; exalted, magnificently dressed, but also naked, blind, mutilated, perhaps enslaved. There are pieces so lifelike that they might be portraits of real people. And there are animal portraits too, full of energy and humour: a cat attacking a snake, two llamas playing, lizards, dogs, centipedes, and spiders.

Moche pottery is also renowned for the confidence and wit of its eroticism. Here is a man gazing upwards, in amazement, pride, or disbelief, at his erect penis which rises as far as his forehead; it's a drinking vessel which you could use only by taking his penis firmly in your mouth. Here is a view of the erotic from beyond the grave: a skeleton masturbating, while another skeleton waits with her hand out for the moment of orgasm. Scene after scene of fellatio and sodomy, the education of generations of wide-eyed Peruvian school-children.

Not far from the deserted battlements of our hotel are the ruins of the Chimú capital of Chan Chan. This was the largest city in pre-Hispanic Peru, but after the strength and solidity of Chavín it looks almost insubstantial now. From a distance the ruins have no shape or order. They sprawl across the desert, like the industrial flotsam that stretches mile after mile beyond the great North American cities.

Historically Chan Chan depended on irrigation for its wealth. So long as its control of the water-supply was undisputed, the elite members of its population seem to have lived peacefully and in style. The massive walls, built entirely of dried adobe bricks, still standing nearly thirty feet high, were not built for defence, but, more domestically, to stop outsiders peering in.

Once inside the walls you find yourself in a privileged area of spacious courtyards, narrow streets, houses, and labyrinths of corridors. There's a reservoir which once would have watered the gardens, but is now just an empty hole in the ground. But the adobe friezes are still young and full of humour. A great wave of fish ripples all the way down the length of one wall, while below there's a line of hungry pelicans waiting to gobble them up.

A few miles to the north of Chan Chan is Trujillo's port of Huanchaco. E G Squier, who had seen almost everything in

Latin America, came here when it was a fashionable resort in the nineteenth century. He was a cultured man and he wasn't impressed. For him, Huanchaco was the 'worst of all the so-called ports of Peru', a point of view many sixteenth-century travellers would have accepted. If it was unattractive from the sea, Squier went on, it 'was hardly less so when viewed from the shore'; and he finished off his visit by talking to a port official 'who occupied a house which was rather stylish for Huanchaco, but which would hardly be dignified by the name of hut in many parts of the world'.

He wouldn't have liked it any better today. Huanchaco, unusually for Peru, is booming. It's in love with its tourists, who are in love with the fantasy that this was only yesterday the romantic fishing village of their dreams. It's a great place if you like fish. You can eat it everywhere. Fish-soup, fish-stew, fish-steaks, fish-kebabs. The beach is dirty, the waterfront hums with overflowing rubbish bins. You can't swim, because the Pacific is far too cold here. But you come to have fun. There are Peruvians from the south in large numbers, especially from Lima. It's like Blackpool and Southend – a messy, happy, candy-floss world, with paper hats and pink ice-creams.

As we sat on the promenade in the late afternoon, the sun appeared for a moment, bringing a reminder that this is a place only ten degrees south of the equator. The brightness played over the high wall of the desert, over the sea, which suddenly came to life, and the church with its sign saying 'Huanchaco Aprista', over the old men fishing along the jetty and the young women, shoulder to shoulder, ruthlessly disciplined in tight skirts and high heels. Then the fog drifted back and the light turned pale again, like milk strained through layers of gauze.

The only thing Squier enjoyed on his visit to Huanchaco was the sight of the *caballitos*, the little horses of the sea. These reed boats, he wrote, are 'probably the most novel craft that the world has ever seen'. Before the Spanish came they were used for sea-fishing by all the coastal Indians of Peru. They appear on Moche pottery and they're still here today. Drawn up out of the water and up-ended, they look like old-fashioned sheaves of wheat at harvest time.

The *caballitos* were also used inland in Peru, as this charming account by Garcilaso confirms:

A single Indian propels each of these boats. He places himself at the end of the stern, lying with his breast on the boat and using his arms and legs as oars. The boat drifts with the current . . . If they are ferrying a man, he lies face downward the length of the boat with his head towards the ferryman. They bid him grip the ropes and bury his face in the reeds and not lift his head or open his eyes to look at anything. I was once passing in this manner across a very swollen and fast river . . . and the Indian boatman went to such lengths in insisting that I should not raise my head or open my eyes that I, being then only a boy, was terrified lest the earth was going to collapse or the skies fall in, and I felt the desire to look up in case I should see something marvellous from the other world. When I felt we were in the middle of the river, I therefore lifted my head a little and looked up at the water, and I really felt we were falling down from the sky. This was because the great gush of water and the furious speed with which it drove the reed boat turned my head. I was obliged by fear to close my eyes, and to admit that the boatmen are right in telling passengers not to open them.

From Trujillo we took a bus north to Pacasmayo along the Pan-American highway, and then eastwards into the Andes again, following the valley of the Jequetepeque river. The road takes you to the mountain city of Cajamarca. Everyone who travelled in north-eastern Peru in the sixteenth century passed through there. For the Incas it was the gateway to Quito and the northern empire, while to the east it controlled the road that led to Chachapoyas and Moyobamba, at the edge of the known world. Cajamarca was also the place where the course of modern Peruvian history was settled by the victory of Francisco Pizarro over the Inca king Atahualpa.

It was easy travelling, in a bus that was almost empty. But then, as the moon was rising in the early hours of the morning, the bus slowed, coughed, and came to a halt. The driver got out and lit a fire by the roadside and we settled down to wait. I remembered coming back to Cuzco by train from Machu Picchu on a night of full moon like this. Close to, the land was bloodied by the fires of the engine and, further away, it turned silver as the moon picked up the lakes and the mountains above the snow line. But the mountains here are lower and the nights are without frost and without drama. After a few hours the driver appeared, oiled and victorious. The bus shuddered off its lethargy, blowing a vast cloud of smoke over the dying embers of the fire, and at dawn we were on the heights above Cajamarca.

# FOUR

We sat in a corner of sunshine, on the summit of a hill called Santa Apolonia, overlooking the city. Ragged clouds edged across the valley, passing on to darken the mountains beyond. The city below was quiet, yielding, from time to time, to familiar noises: of children crying, a car door slamming, the call of the fruit-sellers on the square. Cajamarca looks assured, very European, a place where people might go about honest business without ostentation.

Cajamarca was a great Inca city, but its past seems far away. You might be closer to it reading a history of Peru by the fireside on a winter's evening. Even the modern statue of Atahualpa, placed here to dominate the city he once failed to defend – even this late act of recognition seems a travesty. In his plumed head-dress he looks like the last of the Mohicans, almost charming in his fierceness, a mere icon of the dispossessed.

The story of the Spanish conquest of Peru has been told many times. But it never loses the unreality that is part of all truly extraordinary stories. I once read a book about the Athenian expedition to Sicily in 415 BC – a characteristically Greek affair, spurred on by a duplicitous oracle, and ending in a disaster from which Athens never recovered. I remember that the author of the book said he could never read the story without wishing that, just once, it might have had a different ending. It's easy to feel the same about the story of Cajamarca.

This isn't romance. Little of what we know about the Incas would make us romantically involved with them. It's the inevitability of what happened at Cajamarca that seems so strangely out of proportion, the knowledge that in this meeting of two high cultures there was only ever going to be one result. We cannot expect history to be just, but it's disconcerting to discover it can be as one-sided as this.

Francisco Pizarro and his men arrived in Peru in 1532. They spent some time exploring the coast. Then, in November, they moved inland. There were 168 of them, 62 men on horseback and 106 foot soldiers. In a few months they went on to overcome an empire that stretched nearly 3,000 miles, from Central Chile to the south of modern Colombia. And they achieved this victory in the high country of the Andes, where they were strangers and their opponents totally at home.

The reasons for the Spanish success will always be a subject for discussion. Pizarro was clever, ruthless, and courageous. But his adversary was no less so; and Atahualpa had a fine army, with recent battle experience on the northern frontier of the empire, as well as a group of outstanding commanders.

Atahualpa was outside Cajamarca late in 1532, pausing on his way down to Cuzco. He knew of Pizarro's movements, but he saw no need to worry about the presence of a handful of strangers. He sent out an envoy to investigate and invited Pizarro to come and meet him. Pizarro agreed. The Spanish came down into the city and the Indians allowed them to occupy the main square, now the Plaza de Armas. Atahualpa remained outside Cajamarca with at least 40,000 soldiers until, towards sunset on 16 November 1532, he descended to greet the Spanish leader. He brought a personal bodyguard of between 5,000 and 6,000 lightly armed men, leaving the bulk of his army out on the plain.

For Pizarro's soldiers, Atahualpa's descent was an event of visual splendour and pure terror. The Inca had the material means to impress and what must have seemed a theatrical sense of the occasion. Hernando Pizarro described the scene from the Spanish side:

[Atahualpa] arrived in a litter, preceded by three or four hundred liveried Indians, who swept the dirt off the road and sang . . . [He was] surrounded by his leaders and chieftains, the most important of whom were carried on the shoulders of underlings . . . When Atahualpa reached the middle of the square, he remained standing and a Dominican monk . . . went up to him to inform him that the Governor [Francisco Pizarro] awaited him in his apartment . . . The monk then told Atahualpa that he himself was a priest and that he had been sent to teach the Christian religion. He showed Atahualpa a book which he was carrying and said that it contained the word of God. Atahualpa asked for the book, threw it on the ground, and said: 'I shall not leave from this place until you have given me back all that you have taken from my country. I know who you are and what you want . . .'

Whatever Atahualpa may have meant by these last words, it was an unmistakable declaration of war. The Spanish immediately opened fire with their harquebuses and charged into the Indian forces. For the first time in the Andes the Indians confronted the power of European guns and cavalry. The massacre continued for two hours without interruption. Since Atahualpa's personal bodyguard contained many of the greatest Inca lords, the slaughter quickly carried off the elite of the empire. Thousands died; shot, hacked to pieces, or trampled underfoot as they tried to escape from the square. Those who survived to reach the plain outside the city found themselves at the mercy of horses operating in ideal conditions. The Spanish suffered not a single death.

There have been many massacres like this in the history of the world, but few with such immediate consequences. This was not to be the end of all Indian resistance, but from here on Peru would be Spanish, the wealth of the Incas would be diverted across the ocean, and Spain would have an immense advantage in her struggle for mastery in Europe.

Francisco Pizarro reserved for himself the honour of taking

Atahualpa prisoner. It's impossible to imagine the Inca's response: he was a highly intelligent ruler, hardly innocent or naïve. He must have felt an extraordinarily personal sense of failure in having been wrong about so important an event. His scouts had tracked Pizarro's force all the way up from the coast, through the rough country of the Andean foothills where, at almost any point, they could have been ambushed with little risk. But how could he have guessed that the arrival of these 168 strangers was to be a meeting of worlds, he who thought himself master of all that was known?

The Spanish chroniclers show us Atahualpa lost in wonder at his fate. He admitted that he had planned a savage end for his enemies. He intended to sacrifice some of them to the Sun and to castrate others for service in the royal household. 'Half smiling', he said he had wanted to capture Pizarro, 'but the reverse had happened, and for this reason he was so pensive'. He was crafty enough, however, to try to bargain for his life. He already understood that the Spanish cared more for gold than for anything else in the world and, in a famous gesture, he offered to fill a room with gold, from floor to ceiling. When you come to Cajamarca today you can still see the *Cuarto del Rescate* (Ransom Room), though it's almost certainly the place where Atahualpa was held prisoner, rather than the room he ransacked an empire to fill.

A room filled with gold: it's not the detail or the quantity that fascinate, but the power behind the act. So, even though there's nothing left to see, the *Cuarto del Rescate* is still a haunted place. It's the only Inca building to survive in this most Spanish of cities.

On the day we went to visit, the rain fell in torrents and there was only a small group of Peruvian tourists gazing at a plaque on the wall and arguing about the meaning of what they'd come to see. Even in the late 1540s, when the chronicler Cieza de León was in Cajamarca, he reported that 'all the buildings of the Incas . . . are . . . in pieces and utterly ruined'. Within ten years of the Conquest the Inca empire had faded to a set of broken monuments.

Atahualpa probably guessed that Pizarro would never let him live. But he waited, while the temples of the Coricancha at Cuzco and Pachacámac on the Pacific Coast were looted to fulfil the ransom. He learnt to play chess. In the end, however, he took refuge in superstition when he saw that there was no other way out. Seven years before, when his father Huayna Capac had fallen ill, strange signs had appeared in the sky, and this had led the *amautas*, the wise men of the Inca state, 'to foretell not only the death of the Inca . . . , but also the destruction of his royal blood and the loss of his kingdom.'

Now, in Cajamarca, men again saw a sign in the sky and Atahualpa seemed to accept his fate:

> When Atahualpa heard that the Spaniards were looking at [the sign], they say that he asked to be taken out so that he could see it also; and when he saw it, he became sad, and continued so during the next day. And when the governor don Francisco Pizarro asked him why he had grown so sad, he replied: 'I have seen the sign in the sky, and I tell you that when my father . . . died, another sign like that was seen.'

The Spanish finally offered the Inca the choice of death by burning as a pagan, or by garrotting as a Christian. As night fell on 26 July 1533, Atahualpa was brought out into the great walled square of Inca Cajamarca. He resolved on conversion, since, if his body was not burned, he could continue to believe in life after death. He was christened Francisco, after Pizarro, and, as the Spanish prayed for the salvation of his immortal soul, they strangled him. His body was left overnight in the square, so that all would know of his death, and the following day he was buried.

Observers ever since have debated the fall of the Inca empire and the ease with which the Europeans took over. Obviously, the superiority of European technology was crucial in the early days of the Conquest. But historians have argued that, in the long run, it could not have carried the day alone. In Chile, for example, the Indians learned to use cavalry themselves and, by the end of the 1560s, they were just as skilled on horseback as the invaders. They stopped growing their traditional maize and planted European wheat and barley – crops which grow faster and so were less vulnerable to the scorched-earth policies the Spanish pursued in the summer months of campaigning.

So now it is often said that the Incas failed because they could not adapt. The state was too heavy on their shoulders. Power was too centralised, so that when Atahualpa was seized a vacuum was created that could never be filled by the Indians themselves. Inca bureaucracy ensured that no one in the empire went hungry. But it left the Indians open to the challenge of the unexpected: 168 Spaniards who arrived in Peru with ideas of their own. According to this view, there's no value in thinking of morality and who should have won. All that counts is the reality and who did.

From Cajamarca there is, and has always been, just one road for travellers going east. It runs for about 200 miles, through the town of Celendín to Chachapoyas. All the soldiers moving down towards Santa Cruz de Saposoa came this way and Pedro de Ursúa did the journey at least twice. On the second occasion he spent six months in Chachapoyas, buying supplies and equipment from the local merchants. So the road was probably well travelled.

Chachapoyas marked the eastern limit of the Inca empire. Beyond it lay what the Incas themselves called simply the hot lands (*Rupa-rupa*). In Aguirre's time the Spanish had pushed the frontier of Peru further east to Moyobamba and that was to be the edge of their world for a generation and more. Even the usually phlegmatic Garcilaso has only a traveller's tale to flesh out the reality of the jungle beyond. There are, he says, rumours of 'other extensive lands and provinces stretching eastward [beyond Moyobamba], but it is a land of such great forests, lakes, and marshes that it is almost uninhabitable, and the few Indians who live there are so brutish and beastly that they have no religion or civilization, but eat one another, and the region is so hot that they cannot wear clothes and so go naked.'

Today the journey by road from Cajamarca to Chachapoyas is long and tiring. There is a bad stretch of about ninety miles beyond Celendín, where the road crumbles almost to nothing and few people ever travel. But it's a spectacular route. It crosses the Río Marañón, the river which later in its course Peruvians call the Amazon.

There was only one bus from Cajamarca to Celendín and it was old and dirty. It smelled of stale tobacco and scraps of forgotten food. Everything in Peru declines as you go east. Even the weather. The prevailing winds blow moisture-laden clouds from the jungle and they drop their rain and snow over the first heights they come to. The bus leaked from the ceiling and through holes in the floor and the windows were soon misted over, hiding the increasing greenness of the world outside.

Jane looked around gloomily. 'Whenever I feel homesick for England I think about days like this. Then I'm not usually homesick any more.' She got up and wandered to the back of the bus. There, among a group of silent Peruvians, she discovered two other foreigners, an English woman and her Australian partner. They seemed so different, with so little in common, that it was hard at first to believe they were a couple. Jo was scrawny and looked tough, a butcher by profession, with a half-hearted beard and opinions on everything. Sarah was discreet and delicate, like a dancer, with cropped hair and the palest face.

We saw a lot of them over the following weeks. I liked them both. They'd been travelling together for years. They could mix stories about all the places they'd been with an easy domesticity that was quite unselfconscious. They'd just come to Peru from some troubled corner of the world, but they talked mostly about having children or being ill or losing money. Then, once in a while, they'd remember a riot in Bombay, a hurricane in the South Seas, or an avalanche in the Himalayas.

Sarah loved Peru and Jo hated it. She spoke Spanish well, with hardly a trace of accent, but Jo viewed her talent with deep suspicion. For him it was a bewildering and unnecessary refinement, like being overdressed for a party. He had his own

74

ways of collecting information that didn't depend on strange contortions of the lips and tongue. He would wander over to some serene bystander and say in a loud voice: 'Hey, mate, can you tell me the way to the nearest hotel?' Sarah would look the other way, with her sad, tired eyes; but Jo would come back rubbing his hands and say: 'Yeah, I thought so, it's just over here.' Which, at least half of the time, it was.

Somewhere on the road to Celendín, the bus stopped at a small restaurant, one of those lost places whose only function is to torment the passing traveller. They had lumps of fat and gristle which you could have on a plate with cold potatoes or in a bowl with green soup. We were all hungry, but only Jo could eat. 'Christ,' he said, tearing at a chunk of yellow fat, 'you know one day I'm going to come back and teach this lot how to cut meat. It's not that hard. Mind you,' he went on, 'the fuckin' animal had to have been alive at some point in its history. Nothing you can do with it otherwise. And I've been thinking,' he said, wiping the juice into his jeans, 'I've been thinking that maybe this stuff was dead from the moment it started.'

He finished what was on his plate and called for another helping. He was about to complain about the price, then saw Sarah hadn't been eating. 'Ah, come on,' he said, spooning a mouthful in her direction. 'There's probably nothing better this side of the ocean.' He was always hungry and his body was thin. You could see the lines of his ribs against his sweat shirt. 'Well, the worms get you when you're dead,' he would say. 'No harm giving them a bite while there's still something worth having. It's five years since we left Australia. Just think of the hold they get in five years.'

We reached Celendín to find the whole town celebrating. It was the week of the annual fiesta and everyone was on their way to a bullfight. Fiestas are good fun, but they can go on for a long time and they use up a lot of space in a small town. There was nowhere to stay. The hotels were full, rooms, balconies, and courtyards. Jane and I were setting off to camp out in the country. But at the last minute Sarah smiled her way into a room with four beds and asked us to share. It was a room with no light, no water, and a strange smell. But it was a long time since we'd been with English-speaking people, so we all moved in together.

It wasn't long before Jane got an invitation to a party, an intimate gathering of the Celendín clans. People who were living out their lives in Lima or Trujillo were back for the week to show each other how well they'd done, and they'd taken over the hotel on the main square.

First among the returning natives was a fat, balding man who was supposed to be fabulously rich in ways you didn't ask about. He moved through the party with the ease of someone who could buy anything in the world. He had gold in his teeth and on his fingers. He talked to everyone. He drank. He sang, wonderfully sentimental songs about poor boys and rich girls. He monopolised all the best-looking women, who were too flattered or too afraid to resist. He made them sing too, and, by chance or design, the best singers came first, so gradually the evening fell into tuneless chaos.

In the early hours, when he was very drunk, he recited a poem from García Lorca's *Romancero gitano*. It was about a gypsy who takes a woman down to the river to make love. He thinks she's a virgin, but it turns out she's married. The gypsy has a good time with her, but his honour is troubled at having slept with another man's wife. The poem came across the room in a deep throaty voice obviously reserved for such moments, memorised from beginning to end with nothing out of place. And when he got to the lines:

*Sus muslos se me escapaban*
*como peces sorprendidos,*
*la mitad llenos de lumbre,*
*la mitad llenos de frío . . .*

('Her thighs slipped away from me like startled fish, one half full of fire, one half full of cold . . .'), he went down on all fours, caressing his own thighs as he murmured the word *muslos*.

'Quite sexy really,' said Sarah, pale-faced and dispassionate.

76

But then he leapt on to a table and began to bellow the final lines, as if afraid of losing his way at the moment of climax. He galloped to the end, waved a hand to the loud applause, and collapsed into a chair. Friends gathered round to offer congratulations and he covered his face with a large white handkerchief. Five minutes later, his stomach still heaving out of control, he came back to the world of the living, full of smiles and gratitude.

New people arrived. Jane danced with a German woman, an Amazon with dark eyes and flashing teeth who had just come up the Orinoco from Venezuela. The men gazed, half intrigued, half scandalised, at the swirl of drunkenness and desire. Then moved, with gallant insistence, to restore order. I talked to a woman who was a tax collector in Trujillo. It wasn't an easy job, she said, since half the country couldn't afford to pay and the other half wouldn't. But then she sang and danced as if nothing in the world mattered.

The next day, to cure a hangover and a sleepless night, Jo decided we should go and watch the bulls. The fiesta had been running for four days, which made at least twenty dead bulls. The calculation made me gloomy, but Jo said: 'Ah, come on. It's typical Peruvian. All those people leaping about, sticking their swords into things you can't eat. How can you miss it?'

Outside the bullring a woman was skinning guinea-pigs. She took them live out of a sack, slit their throats, and threw them into a pan of boiling water. Then she skewered them and roasted them over a fire. They looked like baby rats, all feet and nose. Jo and the others disappeared and I waited behind.

'Don't you like bullfights?' the woman with the guinea-pigs asked.

'Not much,' I thought. Then, as the roar from inside signalled the first bull of the afternoon, I said, 'You'd think people would have had enough by now.'

But she laughed and said, 'No one is ever tired of death. I've been coming here for twenty years and I tell you before they had the bulls it was a disaster.'

I stayed and talked and then, when the horses brought the

first bull out of the arena, with its horns shaved and its eyes very knowing and very dead, I decided it was enough for one afternoon.

The following morning we passed by and they were taking the bullring down. It was like the aftermath of a crucifixion. There were stray cross-poles still in place, bits of cloth blowing on the wind, and blood on the mangled grass.

A few days later, with the fiesta over and Celendín almost deserted, we climbed out of town to have a look at the road ahead. It was a hot afternoon, the sky so blue it hurt the eyes. The land was rich and well cultivated, with banks of trees sheltering small farmhouses. Celendín, too, looked neat from a distance, its streets laid out in long, straight lines across the valley floor. We climbed for several hours, until the town was only a few splinters of reflected light in the haze behind us. Then we reached a cold, windy summit and peered over into the void below.

The land was barren and the mountains dusty brown. Further away, covered in rain clouds, were range upon range of gloomy shapes that merged into each other as the land and the sky became one. And far below, a dark green river that sparkled in the light: the Marañón.

It's a symbolic moment for the traveller, the first sight of the Marañón. The river, still narrow and provincial, appears here in a setting that already foretells the monster it will become. Inhuman in scale, the landscape has the power of those landscapes that never change. We stood and looked on in silence. Sarah turned to Jo for the joke that would recover a human dimension, but it didn't come.

To the left was the outline of a rough track that would take us on towards the jungle. It wavered up and down, falling in slow spirals to meet the river. As we watched, the clouds rolled back for an instant and a rainbow stretched over the gorge beneath us. Henry Lister Maw, a twenty-four-year-old British naval lieutenant, came this way in 1828 and described the moment.

> We reached the top of the rugged ridge a little before sunset; and it was from this point we first got sight of the

Marañón. I cannot conceive that anything on earth or water could exceed the grandeur of the scenery; nor do I believe any person capable of describing it justly. The rain was clearing off, whilst a perfect and brilliant rainbow was extended across the river; which, about sixty yards in breadth, rushed between mountains whose summits, on both sides, were hid in clouds, on which the extremes of the rainbow rested.

There's never been a convincing explanation of the name Marañón. When the mouth of what we now call the Amazon was first discovered by Europeans in February 1500, it was named simply the *mar dulce* or Fresh Water Sea, or, even more prosaically, the Río Grande. The word Marañón first appears about ten years later. One of the earliest chroniclers says, 'This river is called the Marañón because the first man who discovered it as a navigable stream was a certain captain named Marañón.'

If that's true, he's never been identified. Others say the name comes from the Spanish word for the cashew tree or its fruit, which in Peru is called *marañón* and is often found along the banks of the Amazon.

The Marañón rises about a hundred miles from Lima and flows north-west through the mountains, parallel to the ocean, for almost the entire length of central and northern Peru. About sixty-five miles from Chachapoyas, it makes a great turn to the north-east. It finally leaves the Andes through the Pongo de Manseriche, a great canyon first discovered in 1557, just below the point where the Río Santiago enters the Marañón from the north. From then on, the river is navigable and settles down to its long course eastwards, through forested plains, to the Atlantic Ocean.

When Pedro de Ursúa's expedition finally moved out of the base camp at Santa Cruz, they began by descending the Huallaga river or, as the chroniclers called it, the Río de los Motilones. The Huallaga rises not far from the Marañón on the northern slopes of the Cerro de Pasco. It runs parallel for the early part of its course, but it makes its turn to the north-east much earlier, finally joining the Marañón about 150 miles east of the Pongo de Manseriche.

Two hundred miles beyond the meeting point of the Marañón and the Huallaga, the river Ucayali flows in from the south. It is from here on that Peruvians call the main stream the Amazon. But for Brazilians this same river is the Solimões (River of Poisons) and it becomes the Amazon much further down, where the Solimões joins the greatest of the river's northern tributaries, the Río Negro.

It's not easy to find a way out of Celendín. The town is at the beginning or the end of a line of communication that runs through Cajamarca out to Trujillo or Lima on the coast. Celendín has always looked to the west, rather than to the jungle. It's been a prosperous town. From the 1860s to the 1930s it had a flourishing hat industry and an English king once wore a Celendín hat to Royal Ascot. But this same prosperity has cut it off from the undeveloped lands to the east.

We spent a week looking for someone to take us on to Chachapoyas, a week hanging about in bars or in silent courtyards, waiting for people who never came. We offered a month's wages to a man with a new Toyota pick-up. He thought about the money for a day and a night, then he thought about the road ahead and his red truck that was the newest thing in Celendín, and he turned us down. Then finally don Francisco, with the saddest brown eyes and the oldest Mercedes in the world, promised to call at our hotel at two o'clock one morning.

His truck wasn't so bad, but it arrived with uncountable numbers of people already aboard. Old men and single women with children. Bundles of live chickens, tied by the feet, which, every now and then, would try to flutter their wings in desperation. There was something about the truck that brought to mind the origins of the New World in slavery and transportation. It rolled with the wind and creaked as if, at the next wave, it would go down without a murmur. And from time to time people would get miserably to their feet and reach out with dignity to be sick overboard.

After five hours of slow descent we crossed over the Marañón on a fine metal bridge and stopped at the village of Balsas. Even in the early morning it was hot and dusty. We bathed in the fountain in the village square and had coffee and stale bread in a fly-blown restaurant. As the name Balsas (Rafts) suggests, this was a crossing point long before the building of the bridge. Here Henry Lister Maw was detained for ninety minutes in the scorching sun, waiting for a raft 'made of about a dozen small trees, of what is called balsa-wood', to carry him over.

In all, the journey of 140 miles to Chachapoyas would take us twenty-eight hours. This is probably the slowest road in Peru, best suited to pack animals, rather than motor vehicles. Jo and Sarah chewed coca leaves to pass the time. But they discovered there is an art to it which they did not know, for it had no effect on their discomfort and left their mouth and tongue on fire.

The truck was too old for the road and broke down several times. In the early afternoon we came to a halt by a narrow bridge and waited there almost until evening while don Francisco removed the wheels and patched the tyres. Jane and Sarah went to sleep in the shade of a tree. Everyone else wandered up and down the dusty track or sat quietly talking by the roadside. No one complained. There was a ruined building a mile or so away. It had once been a restaurant. There was an old magazine on a broken table and shreds of Coca-Cola posters on the walls, with American women in 1940s swimsuits.

The truck moved off again after dark. It began to rain heavily. Don Francisco rolled out an old tarpaulin that reeked of oil and long confinement. We crouched beneath it and the wind and the rain flowed around us, mixing up the unwashed scents of the day. Towards ten o'clock the truck shuddered through a high pass in the mountains and the rain ceased. Here Henry Lister Maw had got down from his horse. He drank a toast and named the pass after his monarch George the Fourth. He'd enjoyed himself along the way. He remembered alder trees, lupins, blackberries, honeysuckle, yellow broom, fern, and heather, 'and an abundance of what the country people in England call buttercups'.

At midnight we arrived in Leimebamba. Jo and Sarah had had enough and we left them, promising to meet up again in a few days. At one o'clock the truck gathered together its weary survivors and in the first hour of daylight we reached Chachapoyas.

Chachapoyas was a booming frontier town in Ursúa's time. Four hundred years later it felt as if it was still recovering. There was a hungover air about everything, the crumbling church on the main square, the cracked paving, the handful of hotels and public buildings, all tired and shabby. There was a plane service into Chachapoyas from Lima even before a bad road existed to connect it with the rest of Peru. Things smell of damp and quiet desolation.

The first person we met was Carlos Domínguez Bobadilla, the departmental director of tourism. He was a friendly, perceptive man, meticulous and informed. In Cuzco he would have been a national asset. Here he was reduced to idleness, saved from ridicule only by an overwhelming integrity. 'I sit here', he said, 'surrounded by a past that is beyond the imagination. There are ancient cities out there, covered by the jungle. Cities larger than anything we have ever seen in the archaeology of Latin America. But we cannot excavate, because we have no money. And you cannot visit, because there is no transport.'

So it proved. There were no buses, no cars to rent; scarcely a road that can't be washed away in a night of heavy rain. The city is cut off, like an island kingdom a thousand miles out in the ocean.

Carlos found us a room in the Danube Café, which spared us the horrors of the hotels. There were tiny framed pictures on the walls and it reminded us of places in English seaside towns. The Danube Café was lonely. It was run by a very nervous woman called Ofelia and her young assistant, a pretty boy named Orlando. No one ever came there. It was, Ofelia often told us, the most respectable place in all Chachapoyas, which may well have been true, though, as the days went by, it was clear the competition for the title was distressingly fierce.

I've never been anywhere so quietly respectable as Chacha-poyas, or known anyone who so cherished respectability as Ofelia. For her it was like a lover, the partner she must once have had and who had vanished: dead? evicted? escaped? unable to bear the sadness of so vast a reputation? She never told us.

'*Gringo*,' she would say to me, 'I believe you have been in Cuzco? They tell me it is not a very respectable place. Now I have no wish to live there, but is it true? You are an educated man and we must learn from you. And *gringo*, why is it so dangerous in Peru these days? Ten years ago you could leave your doors open, go to Lima for a month, and come back and it would all be just as you left it. Now it is terrible.'

I would say, 'I think it's like that all over the world.'

And she would reply, 'It is because there is nowhere any re-spect. Not for the family, not for the government, not for the Church. It is the foreigners who run everything now.'

Then she would look suddenly embarrassed in front of her educated foreigner, and I would say, 'Maybe you're right,' and she'd start all over again.

Ofelia loved sentences that began: 'The great enemy of Peru . . .' The great enemy of Peru was communism; then it was foreigners and the mountains; then, when she found out we were heading east, it was the jungle, because the jungle was full of disreputable people who got drunk and committed fornica-tion in hammocks.

Most of all, I remember the silence of Chachapoyas, and the emptiness. After dark people vanished from the streets; and here, so close to the equator, darkness comes early. The houses had shuttered windows, which gave no light, and the city was ours alone each evening, as we walked out after dinner among the shadows.

We went in search of archaeological marvels. Sometimes we found them, more often not. One day we took a truck called The Lord of Miracles to look for the monumental ruins of Yálape. We spent an idyllic afternoon in a landscape as green as Ireland in the spring, but we saw only a pile of stones that might have been old, and a long, low wall that could have been any age and certainly wasn't monumental. 'You have to hand it to these archaeologists,' said Jane on the way back. 'They know a lot of things we don't.'

Another day, in a small village in the mountains, we were waiting for a lift to Chachapoyas when our driver went to war over a cock-fight and left us to find our own way home in the dark. For two days after that, we searched for the Pueblo de los Muertos, the City of the Dead, which lies only twenty miles north-west of Chachapoyas. From pictures it looks a wild and lonely place, with rows of clay mummy cases gazing out from crevices high in the cliffs. They belong to a civilisation that flourised here before the arrival of the Incas in the late fifteenth century. And they must be extraordinary, but we never saw them.

Of the things we did see, the ruins of Kuélap were the best. They stand high above the left bank of the Utcubamba river, as inconsiderately placed as any of Peru's great monuments, but not hard to find. Kuélap, like the City of the Dead, is pre-Inca and, by that fact alone, largely mysterious. It's a massively forti-fied site on top of a steep hill, engulfed in blue mountains, wide and beautiful as Machu Picchu, but less tended and more secre-tive.

The strangest and least predictable of all our encounters, however, was a human one. We were passing through the vil-lage of Lamud – an enchanting place, ornate and eccentric like nowhere else I've ever seen in Peru. The main square is full of sculpted bushes in various shapes: there's a boat, an octopus, a classic Latin American dictator, a great whale that looks as if it's about to swallow a duck. We stopped to talk to the local priest, Father Alberto, who took us to meet a friend of his, another priest from the nearby village of Luya. The friend was im-mediately recognisable, only a little aged, as Gonzalo Pizarro from Werner Herzog's film *Aguirre: The Wrath of God*.

'The part of Pizarro had been given to a professional actor from Mexico,' he said. 'But I think he was too expensive in the end. Anyway, he never showed up. So Herzog needed someone at short notice. Everyone else was there and they were about to begin shooting. I was working as a priest in Cuzco at the time and Herzog saw me, liked my face . . . It was an odd experience. They made the film in English, which is a language I can do nothing with. Later they dubbed it into German, which I know even less, so I could hardly believe it was me when I saw it.'

Chachapoyas was founded in 1538 as San Juan de la Frontera de los Chachapoyas (Saint John of the Frontier of the Chachapoyas). The Chachapoya Indians had long had a reputation as powerful warriors. The word Chachapoya itself, according to Garcilaso, might mean 'place of strong men'. He says that the area 'was inhabited by many brave people, remarkable for the spirit of the men and the extreme beauty of the women'; he also tells us that the inhabitants worshipped snakes. They were conquered with difficulty by the Incas and later, in colonial times, served heroically at the battle of Chupas, the worst engagement of the civil war.

The old province of the Chachapoya marked a natural limit for Inca expansion. Two days walking to the east and you leave the mountains where the Incas felt at home and enter the high rain forest, which is one of the most unfriendly environments in the world.

The modern road which carries traffic east towards Moyobamba makes a loop to the north, a detour which adds a hundred miles to the journey but avoids the worst of the rough country. However, you can still find the direct route which once linked Chachapoyas with Moyobamba. It begins in lush pasture land, in the village of Molinopampa, then climbs steeply through the last vestiges of the Andes before cutting a trail down into the rain forest. That was the way everyone would have come in Aguirre's time.

We needed a guide, but could find no one who had walked the path in recent years. The school-teacher in Molinopampa said it was heavily overgrown in the later stages and perhaps already impassable. Even at its best, it's hard to believe anyone could have moved large quantities of equipment this way. Not even a mule could attempt the path today and it's a mystery how Ursúa managed to bring his horses down. For the men streaming towards the base camp in Santa Cruz de Saposoa, this was their first experience of the hardships of travelling beyond the old frontiers of the Inca empire.

Eventually, we met a man named Pedro Bacalla and he agreed to take us across the mountains. He said he had done the journey many times in the past. He suggested some things for us to buy in Chachapoyas and we arranged to return to Molinopampa the following Sunday morning.

In the Danube Café, Ofelia was gloomy about our prospects. '*Gringo*, why don't you take a truck to Moyobamba, like everyone else? It's only two days that way.'

'It's no fun in a truck,' Jane said. 'You can't see anything. And they say if you go on foot you can hear monkeys in the trees once you cross the mountains.'

'Ah, but you can hear monkeys in the zoo, *gringa*. Think of it.'

We said goodbye to Ofelia. 'You will find the jungle most disagreeable,' she said forlornly, as we left. 'You know everyone now is on the move. No one stays where they were born. They always want to be somewhere else. That is the greatest enemy of Peru.' She waved to us as we walked down the long street towards the edge of town. And she kept on waving until all we could see was the motion of her red handkerchief, no longer aimed at us or at anyone, just flapping hopelessly in the early morning air.

At a turn in the road we suddenly found Jo and Sarah again. Jo had decided that Peru brought bad luck, so they were on their way to Ecuador. They had just settled into the back of a small truck. Jo was thinner than ever and depressed. Sarah had been ill and looked very white against the Indian faces around her. We talked for a while. There's a special intimacy, childlike and sentimental, reserved for people you'll never see again. We exchanged addresses and plans to meet up somewhere in the future. 'Some place the cow knows its front feet from its arsehole,' said Jo. Then he gave me his hand. 'Be around, mate.'

Their truck pulled away and began to pass slowly around the

city, hunting out the last unwilling travellers. The driver sounded his horn and yelled his destination at everyone he met, as if, even at this last moment, someone might hear the call and find the courage to leave. Each time they came by we waved to Jo and Sarah, but eventually many people had got on and in the end we couldn't see them any more. 'God, they're the real thing,' said Jane in admiration. 'Five years of that. And there was a time when I'd have envied them.'

Pedro Bacalla's house had two rooms. There was almost no furniture. He and his wife and children slept on the dirt floor. There were a few pots and pans, dark from use on an open fire, and an old sewing machine. As we came up, Pedro was repairing the shoulder bag in which he kept his coca leaves. His eldest son Francisco was by his side. He looked about fifteen. He wanted to come too.

The four of us set off across the meadows. Francisco was wearing sandals and carried his things in a flour sack tied over his shoulders with two pink woven bands. Pedro wore plastic workman's boots, without socks or laces. When it rained, which it often did in the days to come, they took out large plastic sheets and stood where they were, waiting for it to clear, or dug themselves into the ground and pulled the sheets over them.

Men were working a patch of forest with their machetes and clearing the undergrowth by fire. We passed a house where hundreds of brightly coloured maize cobs were drying, like washing, in the sun. Small white clouds drifted across the sky. It was warm. The walking was easy and the mountains seemed very far away. We crossed the Río Ventilla. 'It's some years since I came this way,' Pedro said. 'When I was younger, I did the journey several times a year. I worked for a man in Rioja, on the other side of the mountains, and I used to bring supplies for him. Sometimes the rivers were so high you had to walk for a day to find somewhere to cross. Other times you could go anywhere and not even get your feet wet. In a few years no one will be able to find the path any more.'

We forded several streams and then moved out into open country. 'Later this afternoon', said Pedro, 'we shall come to a house. That is the last house for a long time. You could walk for many days to the east before you found another.' Jane liked the way he said *la última casa*. She thought of frontier welcomes, a roaring fire, and an old couple glad to see passing strangers.

It grew colder as we climbed and the wind began to rise. Hours later we came on to a broad stretch of flat land and Pedro said: '*Allí está, la última casa.*' Far away, across the bleak pampa was a low building. As we approached, it vanished in the gathering dusk and when we arrived at the front door it was obvious that it had long been abandoned. This was a bad place to spend the night out, but it was too dark to go any further. The ground was marshy and the floor of the tent was soon dripping with water. Pedro and his son kept vigil around the fire. No one slept. In the morning we cooked maize stew and porridge. Jane put on some dry shorts and a T-shirt and shivered by the fire, her arms locked tightly around her chest. A solitary bird, unrecognisable at a distance, made long, easy passes down the valley, then disappeared into the mist.

We began a steep ascent. It felt harder climbing here than in the western mountains. Perhaps we were carrying more weight in our packs, perhaps it was the increasing humidity as we came nearer to the jungle. Late in the day we reached a pass called simply the Punta de Mojón – the word *mojón* meaning nothing more than a 'landmark' or a 'boundary stone'. From here it is downhill all the way to the Atlantic Ocean, 2,000 miles to the east.

We came off a plateau, following a clear rocky path, and soon crossed back through the tree line. The vegetation thickened and the trail narrowed instantly, scarcely leaving room for one person at a time. Then, without warning, the ground softened, our feet sunk in, and mud began to ooze from under our boots.

The experience of mud in large quantities is always memorable. Soldiers in the trenches of the First World War, faced with bombardment and death, wrote instead about the mud and slime in which they lived, as if it was the only thing that mattered. Its effects are largely physical, of course. After a while, the simple effort of putting one foot in front of the other takes so much energy that it seems hardly worthwhile. But mud induces its own strange psychology, too, leaving you with a feeling of powerlessness and frustration.

Most of all, it smells; a dark, sickly, airless smell. In the beginning, you shy away from all contact, searching for a spot of dry ground on which to place your feet. But after the first mistake, when the slime of centuries pours over the top of your boots or you suddenly plunge up to your waist in a tangle of sludge and decay, then you imagine you don't care any more. You press on straight ahead, disembodied, ignoring what is going on beneath your feet.

As we came down further into the forest, the trees began to close in all around and above our heads. It was as if the outdoor world was left behind and we'd wandered into a windowless office block, where the air never moves and the roof is always leaking.

Vital though the rain forest is to our survival, this doesn't necessarily make us want to love it. It's only too easy to believe that life started out this way, at the bottom of this primeval mire. That's why the reckless fantasy of taming the forest feels so much like progress: stripping the past away for a nice well-ordered ranch, with cattle grazing in the sun.

After another day, the path had almost vanished and from then on we moved very slowly. Brambles sharp as knives would scrape against our arms and legs, or wrap themselves tightly around our packs, holding us motionless. Pedro and Francisco worked a few yards in front with their machetes, their hands always cut and bleeding.

Every day it rained. Sometimes with the roar of a tropical storm, like the sound of an underground train heard from far away; sometimes softly, like the autumn rain in English forests; or softer still, like the snow over northern pine woods. Clothes never dried. Even at night, in front of an open fire, nothing would dry out. Deep inside sealed plastic bags, at the bottom of our packs, there was the same brackish water. Pedro never said much. But he hated the weather and he knew that our supplies wouldn't last as far as the next village.

One night we were forced to camp on a patch of ground hardly bigger than our tent. It rained unceasingly and the mosquitoes bit us through our clothes and whined in our matted hair. We were still high up and the cold descended with the darkness. Pedro told a story about a nearby cave where someone had discovered a statue of Jesus. The man had taken it home with him and the next morning had gone mad. I couldn't decide what the moral of the story was, and Pedro wouldn't say.

Another night, we stayed at a place they called Cedro Huscho (Hollow Cedar Tree). The tree's hollow base was large enough for an entire house. We lit a fire, which quickly filled the space with smoke and brought tears to our eyes, but it was warm and sheltered from the pounding rain outside.

Every clearing has a history and a name, no matter how small it is. In one place someone was remembered for losing a pack horse; in another, a man had once caught an enormous fish. One brief interlude was called the Pampa del Almirante, though who the admiral was who had baptised this scrap of grass and mosquitoes, no one knew.

The complete absence of other human beings in this enclosed area was unsettling. Lying in our tent, listening to the noises of the night, there was nothing we recognised. So much of our ordinary life is spent overhearing others. Most of the time, the scraps we receive from them are so perfectly understood that they pass us by, without comment and without mystery. But this is a world in which there is only mystery and the ordinary seems far away.

Only once did we pass any sign of human presence. That was at Pishcohuaniunan (Where the Little Birds Die). There were a few stones that had formed the base of a *tambo*. A *tambo* is a wayside inn. The word and the tradition go back to pre-Spanish times, when *tambos* were common all along the Inca highways. But this ruin was probably quite recent, for the jungle soon covers everything.

As we grew hungry, Pedro and Francisco foraged for food, without success. The hardwood forests of the northern hemisphere, even the thorn forests of the tropics, are more sustaining than here. In the high rain forest there have never been many vegetable foods and there are few animals that can be eaten. Sometimes Francisco would fire his slingshot at a distant bird. There would be a brief and heavy flapping of wings, and that would be all. Often they would point out something lost in the twilight, a toucan or a parrot. Sometimes Jane would catch sight of it, but I hardly ever did.

In Spanish, they call the high forest the *ceja de la selva*, the eyebrow of the jungle. It's a more hostile environment than the floor of the jungle itself. It receives much more rain and the vegetation is more dense. I told Pedro about a plane that had crashed in the area a few weeks before. Even with modern satellite technology it had taken ten days to locate the wreckage. Francisco was wide-eyed at the news, but his father smiled and said: 'Perhaps it was not meant to be found. And if you could see everything, do you think you could live with yourself?'

I found in Pedro the old farming men I knew as a boy. My grandfather would have recognised the type at once: 'Ah, c'est un malin,' he would have said, as one acknowledging another. Impish, artful, shrewd, and cunning: the whole spectrum of farming virtues and vices. Pedro knew what he knew and didn't much mind what lay beyond. Here only his skills mattered. He was the only one who could find a way out of the forest. Satellite technology could be left to outsiders who needed such things. Besides, unlike us, Pedro had God on his side.

Jane had guessed from the start that he was a religious man. The fact that he used the word *pastor* to mean a clergyman, made it clear that he wasn't a Catholic. Now he told us: he was a Seventh Day Adventist, converted some years ago by wandering missionaries. 'But you see,' he said, a bit wolfishly, tapping his bag of coca leaves, 'I still have some way to go to reach God.'

Finally, late one afternoon, when we had eaten nothing for two days, we crossed a bridge over the Río Salas and climbed up to a village called Pucatambo (Red Tambo). Anywhere would have been welcome. But this was a model village. It was like one of those orderly scenes you see in primitive paintings. On the outskirts there was a large, two-storey house. Washing was drying in the sun. There were three huge turkeys bobbing along a well-made stone path. A woman sitting with wet hair beside a fountain turned away from us, embarrassed to see strangers.

Pucatambo had three football pitches, each one so green it looked as if it had never been played on. You approach the centre of the village down a steep wooden stairway, so that, whatever the weather, you can arrive with clean feet. There is a handful of thatched houses. Everywhere is neat, the grass trimmed and luxurious underfoot. This is a place of quiet satisfaction, dedicated, a little self-consciously, to the timeless struggle of living within its means.

Pedro was happy and among friends. Most of the villagers are Seventh Day Adventists. We met Margarita and her husband Fidel and a large family of sons and daughters, grandparents, cousins, uncles and aunts. Margarita had bare feet. She looked at us and smiled at how tired we were. '*Yo también soy viajera*,' ('I, too, am a traveller') she said and put her arm around Jane. 'Once, when I was a girl, I crossed the forest with my grandfather in both directions, without a break. So I know how far you have come.'

Her house was damp and cold and as dark as the forest we had left behind. We put our packs down on the dirt floor of the communal bedroom and went to wash in the river. It was the time when the men of the village were coming back from the fields. We shook hands with each of them in turn; and, in a moment, the sun was gone.

Everyone ate together in the main room of the house. There was a dull fire smoking in one corner. It gave no warmth and there was no other light. The food arrived from the kitchen and we watched it pass across the fire from hand to hand and on into the darkness. Sometimes orange faces turned towards us as Pedro spoke about the problems of the journey, the weather, the lack of food. At about eight o'clock we all went to bed.

Jane and I slept badly, disturbed by the sounds of so many others around us. I slept in my clothes, because it was cold and I had nothing dry to put on. Jane got undressed in her sleeping bag, tired of the smell of sweat and mud. But she regretted it. She was bitten all over her body and, the next day, the inside of her left arm was a single yellow bruise.

Most people were up before dawn. Jane and I lay, unwilling to move, until Margarita came in and said: 'We are going to raise our voices.' Jane struggled into her jeans just as morning service began. There were hymns, readings from the Bible, a sermon from Margarita's husband. 'And when He comes again, He will separate the saints from the wicked . . . the faithful will enter into life and the unrighteous will go down into extinction . . .' Millennial hopes and fears that belong to a tradition almost as old as the mountains themselves.

Everyone shook hands with everyone else. They wished us a good day and a good journey, and then the men set out for the fields.

A wide path leads out of Pucatambo. Soon we began to lose height rapidly and the wet jungle heat flowed up from the plains below. There were monkeys calling from the trees and, as we crossed the Río Yumbite that separates the department of San Martín from Amazonas, I saw the largest butterfly I have ever seen. It was blue as a cornflower and the size of a small bird.

At eleven o'clock we came to our first jungle village. It was Ofelia's nightmare. There were people lazing about, happily doing nothing in the sun. An old man sat in a rocking-chair on a veranda. A very fat woman swung almost naked in a hammock. We bought some Inka-Cola from a girl. She handed over the four bottles very slowly, one by one, then retreated even more slowly into the back of a darkened room, as if the idea of time itself had yet to reach her corner of the world. We began to see signs of the destruction of the jungle, scenes now familiar everywhere. The blackened stumps of trees and the sense of passing through in the aftermath of an air raid on an un-defended city.

The final day of our journey was very long and very hot. We crossed a wide river, spanned by a broad tree trunk that sagged and shivered underfoot, past fields of rice that looked like schoolbook pictures of China. Then, after bringing us through the forest, where often you could see no farther than a few feet on either side, Pedro lost his way on an open plain. We struggled all afternoon to find an exit from a maze of irrigation ditches. Sometimes we fell into deep water under the weight of our packs, and all the time we sweated heavily in the jungle heat.

It was late in the day before Pedro brought us back on to level ground. I was worn out and lay down under the shade of a pile of felled trees and slept. As the sun was setting, I followed after the others and had almost given up hope of reaching them before dark when suddenly I came across Francisco standing on the edge of the forest. His eyes bloated in astonishment, a stranded fish washed up on the shores of the Marginal, he gazed for the first time in his life at the great highway which connects the Pacific Ocean with the jungle.

The Carretera Marginal is Lima's lifeline to the interior. It's every sort of road. Sometimes broad and smooth, like a North American highway, sometimes narrow and cratered so deeply that a car can disappear in it up to its roof. Francisco watched as two trucks raced each other side by side down a long straight section at a speed that could kill – and this is a rare chance in Peru. The drivers yelled at each other and then they were gone in a great storm of dust.

After our two weeks in the forest this was a happy and sociable time. Soon an eastbound truck stopped and took us on to the town of Rioja, where we said goodbye to Pedro and his son. Then, alone, we followed the Marginal as far as Moyobamba.

# FIVE

. . . é prosiguiendo su camino llegó á un pueblo
llamado Moyobamba.

*Toribio de Ortiguera*

Fʀᴏᴍ ᴄᴜᴢᴄᴏ to Moyobamba, the chroniclers have little to
say about the details of Ursúa's expedition and almost
nothing to say about Aguirre. This is not surprising. Aguirre
was an ordinary soldier. There were many men coming down
through the mountains towards the jungle. They came by different routes and at different times, over a period of nearly
eighteen months. But from Moyobamba onwards, the chroniclers have more and more to tell.

Moyobamba also happens to be the last place on Aguirre's
journey from Cuzco that we can be sure of identifying – until he
appears with the survivors of the expedition off the coast of
Trinidad on 18 July 1561. In between were the anonymous
spaces of the jungle which fascinated the chroniclers and in
which most of the great events of the expedition took place. We
hear ephemeral names, all attached to people, or to things that
happened on the Amazon: the Island of García, the Village of
the Turtles, the Village of the Massacre, the Village of the
Brigantines. But, as with the base camp in Santa Cruz de Saposoa or the shipyard at Topesana, nothing distinguishes these
places from a thousand like them. And it is difficult to see how
the chroniclers could have helped any more than they do. For

once they reached the jungle they found themselves in a land of seemingly endless repetition.

Moyobamba must have been a very small village in Ursúa's time, no more than a few houses. But it had a resident priest named Pedro Portillo, whose involvement in Ursúa's affairs tells us a good deal about the prevailing atmosphere in the months before the expedition set sail.

All the chroniclers agree that Portillo was rich. No one was sure where his money came from. Some said he had saved it through a long period of self-denial; that he went without food and dressed in a manner that undermined his authority as a priest. Ursúa stayed with him on one of his early visits to Santa Cruz and then, on his final journey through Moyobamba, he met with him again.

From here on the chroniclers continue to tell more or less the same story about Portillo, but with subtle variations. It's clear that some of them were trying to protect Ursúa's reputation, while a few were keen to destroy it.

Portillo apparently asked Ursúa why his expedition had delayed for so long, when all the ships had been ready months before. The question would have been entirely natural, Ursúa's reply no less so: he said he had run out of money and couldn't afford to buy powder and shot. Tiribio de Ortiguera, who was not an eye-witness to any of the events and whose chronicle is firmly on Ursúa's side, says that Portillo then made an offer: 'If you were to make me vicar-general of your expedition and of the lands you are to discover and settle, I will provide [the money].' This must be less likely, given Portillo's apparent austerity of character. But the two men allegedly called in a notary and Ursúa departed with 2,000 *pesos*. When he had already spent the money on his powder and shot, Portillo seems to have had second thoughts about the loan, leaving the commander of the fleet in a delicate position.

None of the chroniclers can gloss over what happened next. Those who were on Ursúa's side take the only way out and blame his subordinates: they say he turned to don Fernando de Guzmán, a young nobleman from Seville, who came up with a disreputable plan to get his leader out of trouble.

At that time, one of Ursúa's men, Juan de Vargas Zapata, was lying wounded in a church in Moyobamba, recovering from a knife fight. Late one night, don Fernando sent for Portillo, saying that the man was dying and begging him to come and administer the last rites. Portillo arrived at the church to find don Fernando and some accomplices with loaded harquebuses, and it wasn't long before he had been persuaded to make out a bill of exchange in favour of the merchant to whom Ursúa was indebted.

Then, still half-naked in his nightshirt, he was put on a horse and taken 'out into the Motilones', probably to Topesana, where he was forced to sign away everything, 'so that all he had spent a lifetime acquiring, he lost in a single moment'. After this we hear no more of Portillo until suddenly, on New Year's Eve 1560, he reappears to make a dying speech on the Amazon.

The Portillo affair could only reflect badly on Ursúa's character and leadership. It was a tawdry business, suggesting desperation and muddle. The chroniclers who liked Ursúa hurry over the details, hoping to convince that all was done without his knowledge. Those who were hostile to him, on the other hand, perhaps go further than the truth allows. An anonymous chronicle says that Ursúa was personally responsible for the theft of all Portillo's money; that he forced him to go on the Amazon adventure to keep him quiet, even though he was a sick man who begged to be allowed to stay in Moyobamba. While Custodio Hernández says that Portillo paid for all the expedition's livestock and that he was stripped of everything he had, down to his last chicken.


Today it's all hard to imagine. Moyobamba is asleep. I think some quiet hill station in nineteenth-century India might have been like this. It's always warm but, at nearly 3,000 feet, it's never too hot. Days vanish easily in a shimmer of gentle light and the nights are well regulated, full of the whirring of huge insects that never bite.

Once the capital of the highlands, Moyobamba gradually lost

its place to Tarapoto further east, a town which began its rise during the rubber boom at the turn of the twentieth century and now thrives on the coca trade. All names are cut short here. People say Chacha, Tara, Moyo.

I don't remember how long we spent in Moyobamba. Most of the time we seemed, like the town, to have been hardly awake. My only sharp memories are of dreams. Dreams of the forest, of mud and monsters and darkness. Our only expeditions were down to the river which flows, as quietly as everything else, just below our hotel. We would sit in the sun and watch children playing in canoes and logs slowly floating down on the current.

To the south, the Río Saposoa flows towards the Huallaga river, which it enters just below the town of Juanjuí. Somewhere in this area was Ursúa's shipyard as well as his base camp at Santa Cruz. Like so many other places in Peru it's now a troubled zone. Not long after we passed through, Juanjuí was seized by the guerrilla forces of the MRTA. It was a bizarre propaganda stunt, directed by a former friend of the President, faithfully videoed and later shown to an incredulous public on national television.

If Ursúa had had more luck or knowledge, he would have sited his shipyard further to the north. The Huallaga river is easily navigable over the last 140 miles of its course down to the Marañón. But higher up it is wild, often running through deep gorges. There is a series of forty-two rapids, through which Ursúa would have to pass and which would nearly wreck the fleet. The last of these rapids is a local beauty spot, known to this day as the Pongo (ravine) de Aguirre.


When Pedro de Ursúa came back to Santa Cruz for the last time, he found morale in the camp to be disastrously low. Pedro Ramiro, the founder of Santa Cruz, was Ursúa's deputy there. He had written to his leader months before in Lima, warning him that the soldiers who had been recruited were unwilling to stay much longer and wanted 'to return to Peru'. Saposoa must have been one of the most tedious places on earth and, as the weeks went by and still the expedition had not departed, it is a surprise anyone remained at all.

Ursúa dispersed his men around the neighbouring Indian settlements. This made feeding them easier and reduced the potential for conspiracy. Even so, the risks Ursúa was running were great. This was soon apparent from the actions of two of the best commanders he had, Diego de Frías and Francisco Díaz de Arlés. The former was a confidant of the viceroy, the latter was one of Ursúa's closest friends.

Ursúa sent them, with a party of fifty soldiers, to occupy a settlement variously called Tavoloros or Tabalocos; and he sent Pedro Ramiro with them, because of his experience of the area and his knowledge of the Indians. For some reason they deserted Ramiro on the road, letting him go on ahead while they returned in the direction of Santa Cruz. On their way back, they ran into two friends. They told them that Ramiro was planning to stage a revolt with his fifty armed men and so the four of them agreed to go after him and bring him to justice.

They caught up with Ramiro on the bank of a river, as he was crossing his men by canoe, in twos and threes. They watched, unseen, from a thick patch of jungle and waited until all the men were on the other side of the river, with only Ramiro and his personal servant left on their side. Suddenly they set upon Ramiro, disarmed him, and ordered one of their black slaves to throw a rope around his neck. Ramiro was garrotted and then, some say, they slit his throat. Ramiro's servant, however, managed to escape and brought the news to Santa Cruz.

Ursúa immediately planned his revenge. He left the base camp, at night and apparently alone, and reached the scene of the murder at dawn. He seized the four traitors, with the help of some soldiers who had remained loyal to Ramiro, and marched them back, shackled by the neck and feet. They were formally tried, convicted, and executed. Nowhere in the kingdom of Peru, says the chronicler Gonzalo de Zúñiga, with that touch of finality inherited from the romances of the Middle Ages, was there a man so honoured by the viceroy and all the people as Ursúa.

The incident was a trivial one in many ways. But it reveals a little more about the conditions in the weeks before the expedition took to the river. If we can believe the chroniclers, it shows us an Ursúa who was brave and resolute, unafraid to act against those who were most highly placed or closest to him. It was reassuring, after his failure to punish anyone in the *affaire* Portillo. But the incident also marks the end of Ursúa's old decisiveness. Never again shall we see him act in this way, and all who were with him later, on the Amazon, recognised that they were dealing with a changed man.

Ursúa sent a transcript of the trial of the four men to the viceroy in Lima. He informed the viceroy that all was now ready and requested formal permission to depart.

However, news from Santa Cruz had been flowing back to Lima from a number of sources, advising the viceroy that there were a dozen or so men in the camp who were known to be 'lovers of revolts and sedition'. These men, it was said, had been prominent in the recent bloody history of the kingdom and there could be no doubt as to their identity. It would be fatal to allow them to depart with the rest. It's tempting to assume that Lope de Aguirre must have been one of those under suspicion. But the chroniclers do not name him here and it seems that he had yet to show his hand.

Ursúa's friends also tried to make him see that among the men he had recruited there were some whom it might be more prudent to leave behind. But Ursúa was obstinate. He thanked his comrades for their concern, but he would not move: 'Señores, I fully understand what you are saying and that it is the advice of good and true friends,' he began; 'and I know that these gentlemen [*hidalgos*] of whom you speak are much to be blamed for their part in the past rebellions in this kingdom, and that, in consequence, they cannot be allowed to remain anywhere in Peru.'

But, he went on, it was for precisely this reason that he could trust those under suspicion: 'I believe that they will distinguish themselves on this expedition, on account of the great obligation which they owe to it, since, as they cannot remain in this country, they must seek to discover and settle another . . . where they may live in all honour and repose.' And with that, Ortiguera says, he broke off and would give no further reply.

Perhaps Ursúa was right. If they had gone on to find some little piece of El Dorado, there was a chance the men might have settled down and become model citizens. If they had discovered a place where no one had to work too hard and the fruit fell off the trees, perhaps there would have been a peaceful end to it all. But whatever lay ahead, Ursúa must have reckoned he knew enough about fighting men to keep control of the situation. He'd done this kind of thing before; it was a job like any other. Only this time the scale was different.

The viceroy wrote to Ursúa, giving his permission for the expedition to depart. He advised Ursúa to leave behind the dozen known troublemakers and 'lovers of sedition'. But there seems to have been little urgency in his warning. These men had now left the empire and there was every reason to suppose they would not return. There was no cause for the viceroy to be concerned.

From Ursúa's point of view it was now essential that the expedition should take to the river as soon as possible. A dozen soldiers had already fled, the province of the Motilones had been stripped of provisions, food was getting short. There were, in all, about 300 Spaniards waiting to depart; between 300 and 600 Indian servants, of both sexes; some twenty black slaves, three priests, and a dozen Spanish women, seven of whom were married, or so the chroniclers claim, and five of whom were euphemistically 'in search of a husband'. Separate from all these was a shadowy figure, unnamed by all but one of the chroniclers and forgotten until the very end of the expedition: Lope de Aguirre's *mestiza* daughter, Elvira.

At this crucial moment, just before the launch, Ursúa's lover, the beautiful doña Inés, walked into the camp. We know nothing of the circumstances, but in any age this would have been a romantic gesture. And a very public one. Perhaps, in the best tradition, she said, 'Take me with you.' Was Ursúa angered, then moved by her passion and her beauty to do what no leader should ever have done? Was there a moment when his resolution failed in front of everyone? We don't know. But she won her place on the expedition and the chroniclers believe that this was the beginning of the end for Pedro de Ursúa.

Catastrophe, the future hallmark of the expedition, struck almost as soon as doña Inés arrived. During the eighteen months Ursúa had been roaming the country in search of money and supplies, his men in Topesana had completed eleven ships. Nine of these were large barges, essential for moving the horses and heavy equipment. At the moment of the launch, six of the barges broke up immediately and sank to the bottom of the river.

Toribio de Ortiguera, as a good historian, calmly lays out the possible causes of this immense disaster: the wood was the wrong sort for making large boats of this kind; or the design of the barges was at fault; they had been built over so long a period and subjected to such torrential rains that they had become rotten; or the launch itself had been mishandled.

They were left with three barges and two brigantines. Any prudent commander would have seen the folly of continuing. But Ursúa was too far gone in pride and debt. None of the surviving ships was in good shape and none could take a heavy load. Given his determination to go on, Ursúa made the only possible decision, one whose very absurdity confirms the impossibility of the situation in which he now found himself: he gave orders to abandon almost all the expedition's supplies.

The goats, cows, sheep, and pigs were turned loose to wander in the jungle. They embarked only twenty-seven of the horses they had brought and left the rest – 120 at least and probably many more – to run wild. It was an extraordinary squandering of resources and it meant that, somewhere downriver, starvation was inevitable.

Recognising this, Ursúa decided to divide his company. He sent out one of his captains, Juan de Vargas Zapata, with seventy men. They were to descend the Huallaga in one of the two brigantines and a fleet of canoes. They had instructions to go as far as the mouth of the Ucayali river (then known as the Cocarna), search for provisions, and wait for the rest of the fleet to join them.

This seems a hit-and-miss solution to a serious problem, but it underlines one of the difficulties which all the early travellers on the Amazon experienced. Ursúa had a relative idea of where he was and of what lay ahead, but he had no way of knowing just how far one point was from another. The Huallaga and the Ucayali flow almost parallel in their long journey north to meet the Marañón and they come within forty miles of each other for a time. But the rivers never join, as Ursúa apparently believed they did, and they are separated by the dense forest of the Pampa del Sacramento, which was to remain largely unknown to Europeans until the eighteenth century.

So, without realising it, Ursúa was sending Juan de Vargas and his men on a very long journey. They had to go down the Huallaga as far as its confluence with the Marañón; from where it is still a long way to the point, just below the modern town of Nauta, where the Amazon finally stops its meanderings and straightens out to receive the waters of the Ucayali. How far this is can be reckoned from the fact that, when the main body of Ursúa's expedition followed on in October 1560, it took them a week's sailing to cover the distance between the mouth of the Marañón and the mouth of the Ucayali.

In advance of Juan de Vargas, Ursúa sent out one of his closest protégés, a man called García de Arce, with thirty men in large canoes. They were to go about seventy miles downstream to the territory of the Caperuzos Indians ('the hooded people'). They were to find as much food as they could and resupply Juan de Vargas on his descent. But either because he could find no food, or because he resented his subordinate role in all this, García never waited. He went straight down the Huallaga and, by the time the main expedition caught up with him four months later, he and his men were installed on an island in the middle of the Amazon, somewhere downstream of modern Iquitos.

García de Arce's journey gives us an insight into Ursúa's problems. According to the chronicler Vázquez, the island on which García landed was the first inhabited place he found on all the stretch of river beyond the land of the Caperuzos. All distances here are measured in clichés, but this is a truly awesome journey. Finding food for a thousand people where there were no Indian settlements was to be a constant struggle, on a river which passed through forest so dense that sometimes the men could not even come ashore to rest at night.

The absence of Indian villages over so great a distance is curious. The majority of modern writers assume that almost all the main stream of the Amazon was still densely populated in the 1560s, before the impact of the European invasion began to drive the Indians away from the Amazon itself into the relative safety of its tributaries. But there is no reason to distrust Vázquez on this point; in any case, all the chroniclers have a similar story to tell.

Juan de Vargas followed his instructions to the letter. He left Ursúa early in July 1560, passed down the Huallaga, and, after he had failed to meet up with García de Arce, continued until he reached the mouth of the Ucayali, 'without anything of note happening to him along the way'. At the mouth of the Ucayali he left his brigantine with some sick men under the command of Gonzalo Duarte, and ascended the river by canoe for twenty-two days, until he came to a rich Indian settlement. There he obtained more than eighty canoes and returned with maize and fruit and captured Indians. The journey back down the Ucayali to the brigantines was a harrowing one, and for some reason it took more than six weeks. Three Spaniards and a number of the Indians died and many fell sick.

Having returned to the mouth of the Ucayali, Juan de Vargas and his men set up camp and began to wait. Meanwhile in Topesana, Ursúa laboured to repair the shattered fleet and build new rafts and canoes.

Watching and waiting have always been a part of Amazonian travel and they remain so. But for fighting men they are a disaster. Things once unthinkable in the excitement of departure gradually become the focus for endless unfilled hours.

However Vargas's men thought about their situation, they cannot have been encouraged. For all they knew, they might well have been abandoned. Soon they began to threaten their leader with death unless he would allow them to return to Santa Cruz. They had nothing to do, nowhere to exercise, except for a narrow strip of sand along the river bank, and the crushing monotony of their existence only reinforced the scale of their anxieties.

Juan de Vargas did the only thing he could: he made a speech. He flattered his men. It was only natural that they should be keen to move on. 'But think,' he continued, 'Ursúa has invested a fortune in this expedition. Remember also that we are few in number. It would be cowardice to return home, yet if we go on alone we shall never have the strength to settle a new country. Above all, we must not let Ursúa die of hunger while we have such a store of provisions. Let it never be said in the future that we have been the cause of the failure of so great an expedition.'

So they waited and the weeks went by, until, one day, around the middle of October 1561, an advance party arrived by canoe to tell them that Ursúa was at last on his way.


We left Moyobamba early one morning, following the Carretera Marginal south-east towards Tarapoto. The road loses height with every mile and the weather becomes gradually hotter and wetter. Jane wrapped an old towel around her forehead as a sweatband, looked out of the window of the *colectivo*, and said: 'I think the earth's caught fire.' The jungle was covered in smoke. It drifted across the road and curled around the few passing vehicles, softening distance and perspective. Later a mining engineer told us it came from the spontaneous ignition of underground coal seams. So Jane was right.

Down a straight section of the road, where the car was moving quickly, we saw an enormous snake. There was no doubting its size, because it slithered the whole width of the Marginal, making directly for the opposite side. It looked like a brown river that would never come to an end. All the traffic stopped to let it pass.

We spent five long days in Tarapoto, a town that rose on rubber and now sits complacently on coca. Moyobamba was quiet and reflective, living happily on its ancient past. Tarapoto exists only for the present. It's hot, dusty, noisy, and confined, and it's full of money. A busy street honours the passing of Pedro de Ursúa, but it's overrun by motorbikes, and smells of petrol and rotting vegetables. You wake up each morning to the buzzing of light aircraft on their way to the refining laboratories in Colombia.

Tarapoto might have been exciting once. Now it's only frenetic. It has five radio stations, television, and telex, though 'some essential services ... are passing through a critical period', as the local paper put it, which means, practically speaking, that half the time there's no water. I remember caricatures of men in dark suits and dark glasses, and the spectre of waking lives spent entirely on the telephone.

The women, inevitably, are bored and beautiful. They wander about our hotel, dark eyes, white teeth, in dresses slit up to the waist. They say 'hi' to us in English each time we meet. In the afternoons they take off their dresses and languish by the pool in swimsuits, petulant and abandoned.

At night it's more fun. Insect-eaters crackle from every palm tree and the vegetation seethes under coloured lights. The banal tensions of the day flow into public squabbles as the men come home to the hotel, tired and hungry from their speculative lives. Expecting submission, they find raised voices, the ungrateful slap of hand on cheek. They struggle to understand the depth of boredom in this land of plenty, then withdraw to a place where honour can be satisfied, where notes of pleasure and pain intrude above the whirring of the air-conditioners.

Orders for drinks pass around the terrace each evening, floating aimlessly from side to side, like messages in a bottle. Occasionally, there's a flicker of interest among a massed guard of waiters who look as if they're permanently stoned. The disadvantage of their state is that most of the things you order never arrive. The advantage is that you never get a bill for those that do. We drank a lot in Tarapoto and ate little. Everyone else was sleek and stylish. By the pool, on the dance floor, they all glowed with health. 'I'd never felt so unglamorous in my life,' Jane said afterwards. 'Of course, that was before we got to Brazil. After a week in Brazil you start to wonder if you'll ever feel like a real woman again.'

From Tarapoto we drove in an old truck through a tropical storm to the town of Yurimaguas. There are a lot of jokes about Yurimaguas in the rest of Peru. Its absolute finality makes that inevitable. For it's here that the road runs out. Having already shrunk to a handful of dirt and gravel, often impassable and always uncomfortable, it suddenly ends and there are no more roads until you reach Brazil. If you want to keep going east, you take to the air or the river.

Yurimaguas is the name of an Indian tribe, though this was never their real home. They came originally from further east, downstream of the famous Omagua who once dominated all the flood plain of the Amazon from the mouth of the Napo to the mouth of the Juruá. Modern Yurimaguas is simply a monument to defeat; the place to which the remnants of the tribe were herded after the Spanish invasion.

It's true that it's not much of a town. But it lies at a point where the Huallaga becomes navigable for ships of a decent size. From here there would be boats available to take us downriver to Iquitos, from where it's a week's sailing to the Brazilian frontier.

We were tired and sick after the journey from Tarapoto. Just outside Yurimaguas we had been overtaken by a great cloud of dust. We had watched it from the back of the truck. Sometimes it followed the road, then it would move out over the jungle and suddenly return, getting closer all the time. Moments before it arrived the wind gusted around us, and moments after it passed the rain beat down. The dust was hard and grainy and the wind drove it into every corner. Not even the tropical rain could wash it away.

We found a hotel overlooking the main square. It was noisy in the early evening and there was no water. The supply for the whole town had failed, an event so common in this part of the world that it is completely without interest, though not, given our state, without problems. Jane's face was yellow with dust. She pulled at her hair, absently shaping the matted strands until they stood out from her head like spokes around a wheel. The hotel manager was a cheerful, honest man. He held out no false promises and offered the obvious solution. Why not wash in the river, like everyone else?

The Huallaga here is already wide and sluggish. The bank is steep on the side of the town and it's hard to get down to the water. There were children everywhere, shouting to unseen friends or swimming out to passing canoes. Men on their way home from work stopped by. Women, some as broad and slow as the river itself, carrying shopping baskets and umbrellas held against the evening sun. They would pause a moment to set down their things, then launch themselves feet first, like great ships, into the stream. The river here brings down much silt and a good deal else. As we swam, some children pointed to a large carcass, big as a cow, that turned slowly around on itself and bobbed against the overhanging trees.

Almost everyone seemed to own a colour television in Yurimaguas, which suggested a desperate lack of anything to do at night. Sometimes, on our way back from swimming, we would go into a deserted café and watch the news. Then we'd walk back to our hotel in our wet clothes for another meal of yams and yucca and salt fish; and after dinner we'd lie down and read old newspapers until about eight o'clock, when the electric light dimmed and died.

After that people sat around candle-lanterns and there was only the sound of insects outside and games of cards from the hotel lobby. As the men drank they began to abuse each other, but ritually and without venom. By eleven everyone was in bed.

One night I lay awake in the heat, listening to a couple arguing across the courtyard. They'd left the doors of their room wide open. It would have been unimaginable to do otherwise. They had a room like ours, only it was their regular home. A narrow patch of concrete floor, a bed, and a washbasin that still now, after a week, gave no water. I was never sure of the woman's nationality. She had worked as a prostitute among the gold miners of Brazil and she spoke Spanish with a Portuguese accent, but she wasn't Brazilian. She had settled for a good man in Yurimaguas who didn't care about her past and drank so much he didn't worry very often about the present. After the argument came the whimperings of reconciliation, tired sounds amplified by the emptiness of the night. Words suffocated, heat-logged. 'Don't ever leave.'

Then I thought of all the people who had spent their lives here, never suspecting there were places with cool rooms and the luxury of warm blankets, places that understood the symbolism of a world between the sheets. And I thought of someone I knew in Managua, an American woman whose house I had once shared through the wet heat of a Central American winter. She used to sit out by the road at night, when it wasn't raining, trying to mop up the sweat with a tattered piece of blue cloth she carried between her breasts. On evenings when she was expecting her lover, she would rock back in her chair, roll her eyes, and say: 'Oh God, it's hot.' As if it explained everything. Her unhappiness, her hatred of the tropics, her weariness of life.

Each night in Yurimaguas was worse than the last. I would sleep for a couple of hours, then wake up in a chaos of unresolved dreams, haunted by the smell of the river water that we carried everywhere with us. The bed sank almost to the floor and when you crossed the room at night there was a crunching as of autumn leaves as cockroaches struggled to escape from under your feet.

I tried to imagine Ursúa's great expedition, this *armada* that sometimes seemed so powerful in the hands of the chroniclers. But the pure ideals of conquest or of freedom must have quickly weakened in the face of so much physical discomfort. The expedition was perhaps already half a rabble when it reached this lonely town that was then no more than an even lonelier bend on the river. The soldiers, too, must have been sickened by the river's smell, depressed by the neverending heat; and there can have been few among them who remained convinced of the proximity of El Dorado.

Even so, some might have felt relief on taking to the river, after dragging themselves across mountains and forest, and all the waiting that followed. But others on the expedition, more observant or better informed, must have realised that the Amazon is not a river like the rest, and that the possibility of return was only an illusion. Their ships, once launched, could never hope to sail back against the current. Francisco de Orellana and his men had found that out twenty years before. Searching for the Land of Cinnamon, they had started from the Pacific shoreline in February 1541, to end up, eighteen months later, sailing involuntarily into the South Atlantic.


'It was a sight to behold the happiness and joy of everyone when the longed-for day arrived . . .' So Toribio de Ortiguera imagined the moment of Ursúa's final departure from Topesana on 26 September 1560. His lyricism is unmatched by any of the eye-witnesses. They, on the contrary, hint at disaffection and the prospects of open rebellion. Everyone was forced to go, whatever their state of health or inclination. For if anyone had stayed, he would have become a rich man overnight, on the proceeds of the abandoned horses alone.

They now had the two brigantines and the three barges that survived from the original fleet, plus more than 250 rafts and canoes that had been hastily assembled. The rafts were very large: Custodio Hernández describes them as being as tall as a house, with a raised canopied area where meals could be cooked and supplies stored. They were directed by a long pole fastened at the stern. Versions of the same design, hardly changed, can be seen on the Amazon today.

It wasn't much of a fleet for a journey of 3,000 miles. But presumably in the beginning no one imagined they would have to go so far. Ursúa had all the nails and ironwork removed from the sunken ships, for re-use later on, if the occasion arose.

Which it did, early in the New Year. Only by then Ursúa was dead and command of the expedition was already slipping into the hands of Lope de Aguirre.

On the first day out from Topesana, they travelled only a mile or so, and on the next they passed through the Pongo de Aguirre, the final gorge on the Huallaga. They had now left the mountains behind for ever and 'entered into the Plains, which continue as far as the North Sea [the Atlantic Ocean]'. On the morning of the following day, one of the brigantines struck bottom and lost part of her keel. They plugged the hole with bundles of cotton cloth and passed on into the territory of the Caperuzos Indians. At three o'clock each afternoon they would stop and, if they could find a place to land, they would come ashore to cook their food and spend the night; for they feared the river in the dark, with its floating trees and sudden changes of current.

On 10 October, two weeks after leaving Topesana, they reached the Marañón, which the chroniclers call the Río de los Bracamoros, since it passes through a province known to them as Jaén de Bracamoros. The Marañón seemed to them 'very wide and powerful, twice the size of the [river] they had just descended'. Here they rested for a while, for it had been a difficult period. Many of the rafts had simply fallen apart in midstream, leaving the men to face death by drowning. 'And all day and night it never ceased to rain,' says the chronicler Zúñiga; 'and in this way we continued to have rain for the whole year we spent on that river, and the weather never turned fine for us, scarcely even cleared, except for a few days.'

Ursúa sent out two canoes with some of his best harquebusiers to look for food. In two days of searching they found nothing; so they travelled on. On 19 October they reached the confluence of the Marañón and the Ucayali, where they found the faithful Juan de Vargas with his men. They had been waiting so long for the main expedition that most of the food they had brought down the Ucayali was now exhausted.

For once, however, the river was kind. There were turtles and turtle eggs; birds, about the size of young pigeons, easy to catch and good to eat; ducks and turkeys and alligators, which they shot with their harquebuses.

They camped out here for a week. They abandoned many of their rafts (for even the serviceable ones were growing heavy in the water and slowing down the rest of the fleet) and transferred to the canoes which Juan de Vargas had brought down from the Indian settlement on the Ucayali.

Almost as soon as they moved on down the Marañón, one of the brigantines hit a log and began to founder. By rowing hard, they managed to beach her and salvage the cargo. But the ship was beyond repair and had to be left behind. Again they re-distributed men and supplies, so that the expedition was now more dangerously overloaded than ever.

Luckily, they had reached calm waters. Once the Amazon comes out of the mountains, it loses height very gently. Manaus, in Brazil, for example, is a thousand miles from the sea, but it lies only about a hundred feet higher than Belém near the river's mouth. While ocean-going ships can reach up the Amazon as far as Iquitos, more than 2,000 miles from the sea. So the fleet survived in ideal sailing conditions, and carried on down a river that had become wide and placid.

Keeping to a course, however, is not always so easy. Often they found themselves running between islands, where the river splits into parallel channels. New streams, from among the 11,000 that drain the Amazon basin, enter all the way down on either side to confuse the steersmen. They kept to the right bank, which became more difficult the further they went and the more the left bank receded; until finally, twenty days' sailing from the Atlantic, they lost sight of the left bank altogether, as the river broadened out to become half as wide as the English Channel at the Dover Straits.

One afternoon they came across some Indians fishing from their canoes on a deserted beach. The Indians had gathered more than a hundred turtles, which they left on shore as they fled, astonished, up a narrow stream. But for many days there was no other sign of human life.

On 3 November they reached the mouth of a river that Orti-guera calls the Zamora, Vázquez the Río de la Canela (the river of cinnamon), the Incas the Napu, and which today is called the Napo. It enters the Amazon from the north and the presence on board of Alonso Esteban, one of the survivors of the Orellana expedition, enabled Ursúa to identify it as the river by which Orellana and his men had descended in 1541-2.

The following day they reached an Indian village set on an island in the stream. Here, to their immense surprise, they found García de Arce, Ursúa's protégé, who had been sent out from Topesana four months earlier with a foraging party.

García and his men had suffered badly on their journey downriver for reasons that were becoming all too familiar. Food had been scarce all the way. Not only had they found none to resupply the main expedition, but they themselves would have starved without García's skill as a harquebusier. They had survived on alligator meat, and had lost two of their companions who had wandered off into the jungle in search of food and never returned. Ortiguera estimates that they had travelled 300 leagues (about a thousand miles) beyond the land of the Caperuzos without coming across a single Indian village.

On the island of García, as the soldiers quickly named it, there was at least something to eat. Exactly what, and how much, isn't clear. Zúñiga, who, after all, was there but was inclined to exaggerate, says the only food to be had was manioc and sweet potatoes. Ortiguera, who was not there, but who seems to have had reliable informants, says there was good fishing, maize and yams, turkey and duck. From sweet manioc the Indians made cassava bread 'and a sort of drink which is delicious and refreshing . . . and which even intoxicates like wine'.

About one thing, however, there is no doubt at all: the arrival of García and his men had spread terror through the Indian population. The Spanish were fearful for their lives and used their technological superiority in the crudest way. They set up a wooden stockade in front of the village and retired behind it to fight off Indian attacks from the river. García, *maravilloso arcabucero*, one of the finest marksmen in the expeditionary force, once brought down five Indians in a canoe with a single shot.

On another occasion, the Indians had come seeking peace and

García, fearing an attack, had driven forty of them into a hut where they were all put to the sword. This last incident is significantly condemned by Ortiguera, who shows himself much closer to the official, civilising policies of the Spanish crown than to the brutalised attitudes of the frontiersmen who are the subject of his story. The Spanish, he writes, acted 'with great cruelty', since the 'wretched Indians' did not deserve such treatment: 'they are people of good disposition' (*de buena digestión*), as they had shown twenty years before, through the friendship they had offered Francisco de Orellana and his men. Orellana's party had come through here, sick and weak with hunger. The Indians had saved them, and, 'without ever having seen a Spaniard', they had helped them build a brigantine to send them on their way.

The chronicler Francisco Vázquez also tells the story of García's massacre of the forty Indians. He would have had it at first hand from his companions and his is the authentic voice of the frontiersman. He gives the details, but without indignation. This was war; only those safe at home, with no experience of what conquest was like, could enjoy the luxury of moral reflection.

But at the same time, Ortiguera's point was more than a simply moral one. He observes that by lapsing into a policy of terror as their only way of confronting cultures they did not understand, the Spanish were creating problems for themselves all the way down the river. Almost everywhere they went in future the Indians would flee before them, leaving their villages deserted, 'which caused them not a little difficulty', says Ortiguera, 'since they would meet no one from whom they could obtain information that might be to their advantage, nor anyone who would give them the things they needed'. Through their actions the Spanish were isolating themselves in an alien environment where, above all, they would need support and advice.

Relations between the Spanish and the Indians improved after Ursúa arrived with the rest of the expedition. The Spanish indulged in some minor trickery, trying to barter plates of tin and pewter as though they were silver, and copper frying pans as though they were gold. The Indians here wore fine cotton clothes, hand-painted in various colours, with golden ornaments in their ears. They did not eat salt and, when given it to taste, they spat it out in disgust. The Spanish were to be much troubled by the lack of salt on the river; the only seasoning they came across until they were near the Atlantic was the chili pepper. This, could they have known it, is an important source of vitamins in the jungle, but it was no more to their taste than salt to the Indians.

Ortiguera calls García's island the *isla de los Cararies*; the village, he wrote, was divided into two *barrios*, each containing about thirty houses, with each house providing space for between fifty and sixty people. Though his observation is at second hand, it accurately reflects the bipartite organisation that was, and remains, characteristic of many tropical forest communities.

Here the horses were disembarked for the first time since leaving Topesana. Two or three had already died and it is extraordinary that so many still survived. The absurdity of bringing them downriver, while abandoning the livestock, must by now have been apparent to everyone. The horses could add nothing to the expedition's prospects. But the cattle, sheep, and goats might have been its saviour, if the party had ever gone on 'to discover and settle' new lands. The Indians of the New World generally had no way of turning grassland into food and in this the Europeans had an immense advantage. In all those places where it was too hot, too dry, or too wet to grow crops, livestock was the key to a comfortable existence.

They rested on García's island for a week. It was here, according to Vázquez, that they first began to be troubled by mosquitoes, an interesting observation, since there is a tendency to imagine that Amazonia has always been mosquito-ridden from one end to the other. Here, too, we find Ursúa making an appointment which, in view of what was to come, was spectacularly wrong-headed: he named don Fernando de Guzmán *alférez general* of the fleet, effectively his second-in-command.

He may also at this time have given prominence to Lope de Aguirre, who must otherwise remain in obscurity a little longer in the pages of the chroniclers. Custodio Hernández says that Aguirre now became Comptroller of the Dead – responsible for the property and personal effects of those who died on the river. But he is the only chronicler to mention the appointment and perhaps its funereal symbolism is too neat to carry conviction.

Ursúa's behaviour seemed strange to everyone and it was obvious that something was wrong. His friends wanted him to send out reconnaissance parties to investigate the Indian settlements that lay along the Amazonian tributaries. But Ursúa was unenthusiastic. Above all, he simply wouldn't command. We can't get close enough to him to know what was in his thoughts at this time. The eye-witnesses were ordinary soldiers, far below his social rank and excluded from his inner circle. Those best placed tell of two possibilities, which, while not mutually exclusive, would be hard to reconcile: that Ursúa was sick, which is entirely plausible, though not very exciting; or that he was in love, in the grip of some fatal passion. Naturally, the chroniclers tend to favour the second of these options, but they have no genuine insights.

So Custodio Hernández writes: '[Ursúa] would govern only with doña Inés at his side, and he loved her so much that without doubt he was lost on her account; and the soldiers used to say it was only possible because he was bewitched.' While this same belief in sorcery appears in Vázquez's account of events a few weeks later:

> And . . . [the soldiers] would say that doña Inés, his lover, had so worked her influence on him that his nature had changed, and that she had bewitched him; for, where he used to be easy-going and sociable with everyone, he had turned rather grave and surly, hostile to all conversation; and he would eat alone, something he had never done, and he would invite no one to share with him: he had become the friend of solitude . . .

Is this as plausible as the account of Ursúa as a sick man? Ursúa *amigo de soledad*? Ursúa bewitched? It sounds unlikely for a fighting man of his age and experience. It sounds even more unlikely if we imagine the passive beauty invoked by those who were well-disposed towards doña Inés. Yet all the chroniclers suggest she is the cause of Ursúa's downfall and most seem to believe it. So perhaps, after all, it was true.

# SIX

NOTHING IN NATURE is as red as the dye of the *achiote*. You need a sharp knife and then the crushed seeds of the *Bixa orellana* will darken your hands in an instant. Jane lay in her hammock, rocking gently in the breeze from off the river, and drew long lines across her body. She sketched two unequal spirals on either side of her nose, then drew on, crossing the lines beneath her breasts, and down until she reached her feet. She looked at the patterns and laughed. 'I've never used make-up in my life, except lipstick a couple of times when I was twelve. It's a funny place to begin. I think I'm bored.'

We had left Yurimaguas ten days before and we were still a long way upstream from Iquitos. Travelling these great rivers calls for patience and luck. It's like hitch-hiking. You can wait around for ever, hoping for the ride that will take you all the way; or you can settle for anything that's passing – and then you risk ending up like the jumping frog in the riddle, where every leap takes you only half the distance of the previous one and your destination stretches out into infinity.

The large ships that could have taken us to Iquitos in a few days had berthed well below Yurimaguas, because the river was too low. So we took a local boat and now we were encamped, waiting for something else, in a village that was only a couple of huts on a sandbar. Life here was not unpleasant, though, after a while, it was certainly limited. The only food was yams, the occasional pineapple, and what you could catch. We tried for bearded cat-fish, which sting your hands when you touch them, and piranhas, beautiful fish with silvery scales and pretty red markings around the gills. The small ones are just bones and teeth, but if they're big enough to alarm you then they're good to eat.

Our neighbour was a white-haired man who said he was fifty but looked as old as time itself. He shuffled about uncomfortably on bare feet, talked to himself in a language that can never have been made for communication with others. He had a scar from a machete wound that began by his neck and disappeared into the waistband of his trousers. He had a parrot in a cage; it looked miserable and unkempt and he said it was dying. A dying parrot in a cage in the heart of Amazonia: it's curious to have travelled so far to meet with so obvious a symbol as this.

But the evenings were full of life. The sounds of the jungle are truly one of the wonders of the world. You can sit for hours in your hammock, listening to a story that has no end, a story that is also restful because it is without meaning. For us, it was only liquid, random sound, stretching out to fill the vast space of the forest, bringing to the ear the same magnified and unreal sensation that the light in the mountains brings to the eye.

Throughout most of its history, the limitations of Amazonia have been freely accepted by its inhabitants. Only at odd moments have people fantasised about its riches. In the sixteenth century, men searched briefly there for El Dorado, because it was the largest space still left unexplored; while in the days of the European Enlightenment, there were those who claimed it must be rich simply because it was hot. But now, in the late twentieth century, the facts are known and only poverty or greed will try to dispute them.

This is not a wealthy land. The soils are useless for continuous agriculture. Maize quickly strips away the limited fertility. At best there's manioc, the most undemanding of crops. Hunting is difficult in the thick forest and there have never been any animals that could be domesticated for food, unlike the llamas and guinea-pigs which provided the Incas with their protein.

So the small farmers scratch and cut and burn in their struggle to make something out of the land. No one hates the jungle as much as those who live on its edge, the *chacras*, like the gardens of medieval Europe, a symbol of peace and order in the midst of the wilderness. On the verge of darkness, these farmers pursue an ultimate domesticity. There is nowhere to go. Life is a routine sketched out at a pace so slow that everything is retained in memory, a burden to be carried in the hope of better days.

The *chacras* which line the river bank never go far from the water. People here are tied to the river. It's only natural that they should fear the jungle at their backs. Every tree seems to repeat itself, every shape that once seemed strange or surprising returns in ever stranger forms, until all patterns are lost in the vastness of the forest, which is without differentiation.

We describe certain scenes from our urban world as 'concrete jungles': the way odd clusters of shapes reduce us to mere spectators in the face of a greater power. The metaphor is apt. Here, in the vegetable jungle, one is confronted by a reckless geometry that is beyond one's capacity to control. Which explains our passion for destroying it, for sweeping it all away, like the Walrus faced with the multitudinous sands.

The old inhabitants of these rivers have long gone. By the mid-eighteenth century, the main stream of the Amazon was already denuded, along with all the major tributaries. By the early nineteenth century, the choices facing the remaining Indians were simple: they could, in Robert Southey's words, either stay where they were 'and be treated like slaves, or fly to the woods and take their chance as savages'. By the early twentieth century, there was nothing for the nostalgic observer to do but mourn. Here is the missionary Kenneth Grubb:

> These rivers are silent today, except for the lap of the waters along some deserted beach, the hoarse cry of the parrots or the call of the inambu. The past has gone, with its peoples . . ., leaving only that bitter sense of impotence, as of being present before a consuming conflagration and at the same time being powerless to assist.

We travelled on slowly towards Iquitos, changing from one small boat to another. Nothing moved on the river. Only the waves of our boat, running out to the bank, then falling noisily over each other on the return. Sometimes huge trees went by, rolling heavily to their own rhythm, sinister, like drowning men. Today the Amazon is a vast highway, with its service stations, its exits and entrances, carrying traffic over the width of a continent, but with no life of its own.

Only details survive in these monotonous spaces. A man standing like a scarecrow in the heat, struggling to raise a hand in greeting as we passed. Children in school uniform, paddling home in their canoes. And once, near Iquitos, where the thatched houses along the bank already had television aerials, two women crouching in the twilight as they washed their hair. They made a vague gesture of embarrassment, protecting themselves with slow, listless movements of arms and shoulders, then suddenly vanished beneath the muddy stream.

Iquitos first appears from far away as a single, slender spire reaching into the grey rain clouds. Through the binoculars the shape turns instantly secular and drab. It's an unfinished hotel, concrete below with an increasingly informal garden above, where the jungle has reclaimed its rights.

But after three weeks of sweating and waiting, Iquitos is civilisation itself. It has paved roads, hotels with air-conditioning, doctors, and some of the best ice-cream in Peru. It has none of the seediness of the other river towns. Even the corners of its poverty and the hideousness of its vultures are picturesque. There are motorised rickshaws which will take you anywhere you want to go. Not that there's a great deal of choice. None of the roads here leads very far and between breakfast and lunch you can see all there is to see in Iquitos.

Visitors come here because Iquitos is surrounded by the jungle. This fact is the beginning of a series of ironies. We all want our jungle 'real', untouched by boot or machete. We want it virginal; ravishing because unravished, like the secret cove of childhood or the burning sands on which no one else has ever lain. We seek the smell of danger, an encounter with a world where lions and tigers will never intrude, but where we would not think ourselves foolish for believing that they might. And we want it all without having to go too far or for too long.

The tour operators respond to these needs with good will and understanding. Their brochures are full of the promise of a lonely paradise only an hour away, of secluded tributaries where alligators lurk and you can be back in your hotel for dinner. Or else you can stay in a jungle lodge, with air-conditioning and cocktail lounges, if you're rich, or faulty screens and authentic mosquitoes, if you're not. You can even see Indians, for Indians are the archetypal symbol of the jungle, full of strange wisdom and still, in spite of everything, a little fearsome.

Naturally, there are no indigenous Indians left anywhere near Iquitos. Once, in the years immediately before the Spanish conquest, Tupí-speaking Cocama and Omagua came this way, moving westwards into the Upper Amazon from their homelands downriver. A branch of the Cocama occupied the lower Ucayali, while for hundreds of miles to the east the river was dominated by the Omagua.

These tribes brought an advanced civilisation with them. Orellana's party was amazed at the size and number of Indian settlements, the fine roads and, most of all, the beauty of Omagua pottery, which seemed to them the equal of any in the world. But by the early eighteenth century there were only a few hundred Omagua left. Now they have simply merged into the rural world of eastern Peru, like those rivers which dry out in the desert and never reach the sea.

The Indians who can be found today near Tamshiyaco, conveniently close to Iquitos, are Yaguas. One of the tour operators brought them down from the river Napo a few years back and set them up here. There are about twenty-five people in all, divided between three families. They live in a clearing, in a large thatched communal house. They cultivate manioc and bananas and make souvenirs. We talked with them one afternoon. They laughed very loudly when they told their story, and, if they didn't see their life as ideal, they refused to treat it as tragic.

'People who come to visit us are very kind. Very polite. But often it's hard to speak to them because they are so shy. They don't really believe we are going to eat them, but sometimes they give us such a look when they think we can't see. Ooh, and then we put on our grass skirts and dance.'

In our hotel in Iquitos there are some photographs of Yaguas Indians. One shows two women. They sit, almost touching, one behind the other, looking very sadly at something to the left of the photographer. One woman has long dark curls that neatly circle her nipples. The other has shorter hair and much larger breasts. They both look very young, but the camera contrives experience for one, innocence for the other. Their eyes invite the spectator to guess at their extraordinary sorrow. Two wistful sisters and an illusory bridge over worlds.

Iquitos feels a long way from Lima. You can fly there in just over an hour, but before the advent of the aeroplane the quickest route to the Peruvian capital was down the Amazon to the Atlantic, then via Southampton or New York and the Panama Canal. Joseph Woodroffe, an Englishman who came to South America in 1905 and later published a book called *The Upper Reaches of the Amazon*, gives a portrait of Iquitos in the early twentieth century. He remembers his hotel ('the most abominable place in which I had ever in all my life been obliged to take my meals'), the mosquitoes and flies, the dirt and poverty; and he was able to indulge his English fascination with the primitive drainage-system:

> Down the centre of each street or along the sides, where some attempt at paving exists, run the drains which carry off the sewage of the town, at all times of the year an abomination, the more so in the summer when rains are not sufficiently frequent to carry away all the filth and refuse which are thrown into them. You may imagine what this means in a town which I suppose at that time had about ten to twelve thousand inhabitants, and in which sanitary arrangements were almost unknown.

The details are not so curious in themselves. What makes

Woodroffe's account valuable is that he was able to compare his experiences in 1905 with the way the town had changed eight years later. By the end of 1913, it had become 'a fine city, with good drainage, streets, public buildings, hotels, and dwelling-houses'. It would have a great future, he thought, 'when linked up by railway with the Pacific coast' – this being still an age when men believed there was nowhere you couldn't drive a train, given the ingenuity and the capital.

The total transformation Woodroffe observed was the result of the rubber boom, the economic miracle that descended on Amazonia in the seventy years after 1850. For a brief period, the area was almost the only source of a commodity that the world was just beginning to devour in large quantities. In that sense, the miracle was an historical accident, and, like most such accidents, was unsustainable.

The man whose name will always be associated with the history of the area is Julio César Arana; and the man who did much to challenge Arana, though never to defeat him, was the British diplomat and Irish patriot, Roger Casement.

In folk memory, Arana has become the absolute model of the rubber baron. His home was Iquitos and his career belongs to the Amazon's golden years, the period between 1880 and 1910. Arana began as a general trader on the Upper Amazon. But in 1906 he bought a vast estate beyond the Putumayo river, in what is now Colombian territory. In 1908 he floated his Peruvian Amazon Rubber Company on the London Stock Exchange. The bicycle craze of the 1890s and the growing popularity of the motor car meant that a lot of people were prepared to invest speculatively in rubber. Arana looked set for international fame as a respected business man.

His 12,000-square-mile estate contained an estimated 50,000 Indians at the beginning of the twentieth century. They were divided into four tribes, differing in language, but sharing much else in terms of way of life and custom. The Indians lived in almost complete isolation from the Europeans; their culture was flourishing and intact. The region was thus ideal for slaving parties, which began in the 1880s.

124

By 1909 reports of brutality on the Putumayo had spread and the English magazine *Truth* published a series of articles under a headline that quickly became famous: THE DEVIL'S PARADISE. By the following year, English public opinion had persuaded the Peruvian Amazon Company's board of directors to send a Commission of Inquiry to Peru. Roger Casement, who at that time was stationed in Rio, was appointed as the British government's official representative. He began an investigation that would lead to a knighthood for his services on behalf of the Amazon Indians.

Casement had made his reputation in the Congo Free State, where he learned much about the workings of the rubber industry. His approach to the world's problems was a compelling mixture of the intuitive and the systematic. There is a characteristic moment during his time in Africa when he came across a set of trade returns for the Upper Congo. He saw that a great deal of rubber was coming out of the Congo, but that virtually nothing was going in, except guns and ammunition. From this he concluded that the natives gathering rubber in the hinterland must have been working unpaid, for they were unable to buy anything. But he also had the revelation that what he was reading in those columns of figures was a history of modern slavery.

One of the milder ironies of Casement's work on the Putumayo is that he never liked South America. He first went there in 1906, as Consul General for the State of São Paulo, with headquarters at Santos. That town, he noted, had been accurately described by Richard Burton in 1867 as 'the Wapping of the Far West'. Brazilian life in general seemed little better. It was, he said, 'the most perverted, comfortless and dreary of any in the world. The country is beautiful beyond words and the people uninteresting, pretentious shams beyond conception.'

Casement first came to Iquitos in August 1910 ('Very hot at Iquitos and lots of mosquitoes . . . Hotel dreadful,' he noted in his diary). He quickly observed that the stocks were still widely used as a means of punishing the Indians. If that were so in the immediate vicinity of Iquitos, it was obvious what the situation must be like in the totally unpoliced country of the Putumayo.

Reality proved even worse than his suspicions. In his report to the British foreign secretary, dated 17 March 1911, Casement detailed the use of the stocks by Arana's employees:

> Men, women, and children were confined in them for days, weeks, and often months... Whole families... were imprisoned – fathers, mothers, and children, and many cases were reported of parents dying thus, either from starvation or from wounds caused by flogging, while their offspring were attached alongside of them to watch in misery themselves the dying agonies of their parents.

The Indians on the Putumayo were being worked to death, starved, mutilated, burned alive; often beaten so badly that the wounds would never heal and the victim, 'with maggots in the flesh', would be turned adrift to die in the forest. Casement listened and measured. He noted that the leg-holes in one set of stocks were three and a quarter to three and a half inches in diameter; in another place only two and a quarter to two and a half inches. Arana's company, he concluded, was on the way to exterminating the entire Indian population of the region.

For a time, after his return to England, Casement believed that victory was his: 'I have blown up the Devil's Paradise in Peru', he wrote to his cousin; 'the abodes of cruelty are not so secure as they were.' The House of Commons set up a Select Committee to study the implications of the Putumayo affair. Arana himself even testified before it. Public opinion was outraged. But, in the long run, nothing was done. Arana was never brought to justice. In fact, he went on to complete a public career of distinction. He became a senator and died in Lima in 1952, at the age of eighty-eight.

Casement, on the other hand, had only a few years to live after his visit to the Putumayo. On the outbreak of the First World War, he went to Berlin to try to enlist German support for an independent Ireland. When he returned to Ireland in 1916, he was captured by the British and charged with high treason. In June 1916, two months before his death, he received a strange telegram, addressed to him at the Tower of London, where he was imprisoned. It came from Julio Arana:

Am informed you will be tried for High Treason on 26 June – want of time unables me to write you being obliged to wire you asking you to be fully just confessing before the human tribunal your guilt only known by Divine Justice regarding your dealings in the Putumayo business . . .

You tried by all means to appear a humaniser in order to obtain titles, fortune, not caring for the consequences of your calumnies and defamation against Peru and myself doing me enormous damage. I pardon you but it is necessary that you should declare now fully and truly all the true facts that nobody knows better than yourself.

Julio Arano

The jury at Casement's trial were out for less than an hour; the verdict, on the evidence, could only have been guilty. But he still hoped for a reprieve. He had friends. Arthur Conan Doyle contributed £700 towards his defence costs, while the *Manchester Guardian* published a characteristic letter from George Bernard Shaw ('Ireland has enough heroes and martyrs already, and if England has not by this time had enough of manufacturing them in fits of temper, experience is thrown away on her').

Casement was to die a Catholic, the final act of treachery against the cause of Ulster and the final response to the emotional needs of a lifetime: 'In Protestant coldness I could not find it', he wrote, 'but I saw it in the faces of the Irish. Now I know what it was I loved in them. The chivalry of Christ speaking through human eyes.'

The British government refused to allow his body to be returned to Ireland and he was buried at Pentonville Prison, inspiring Eva Gore-Booth to write:

> No cairn-shaped mount on a high windy hill
> With Irish earth the hero's heart enfolds
> But a burning grave at Pentonville
> The broken heart of Ireland holds.

Half a century later, in 1965, he was finally allowed home.

'I have no belief in Englishmen,' Casement had written, nine years before his death. It is ironic to reflect that, in many ways, the Indians of the New World were better served by reactionary Spain than by Anglo-Saxon liberal democracy. Of course, the Indians suffered terribly at the time of the Conquest, not least from European diseases. But the Spanish crown struggled to give them a measure of legal protection, to reduce the degree of control which the settlers could exercise over them.

Forced labour, the evil against which Casement campaigned in vain, had already been abolished by the Spanish crown in 1549. The Aguirre who received 200 lashes of the whip in Potosí was an early victim of the new prohibition, caught up in the battle between the colonists' desire for freedom and the monarchy's desire for order.

Looking back now on the history of that battle, we see how complete was the victory of the colonists. Men like Aguirre came to the New World in search of freedoms denied them by Old World; mobilities of class, of social and economic expectation. The modern world was made largely in their image, a world which implicitly rejected stability, in favour of unlimited opportunity for all who could seize it. Long before Conrad's Kurtz, Aguirre begins to show us the darker side of something that is already ourselves.

That the new world order would be profoundly secular and material was clear to Aguirre. According to Francisco Vázquez, he used to say that 'God [had] reserved heaven for those who wished to serve and the earth for those who knew how to act'; and he would add that we should not be afraid of hell, if that was all that stood between us and our desires.

As old restraints fell away, the modern world found itself backed into an unending relativism. Faced by monsters, we could now do little more than try to measure the extent of the horror, gauging human rights by standards which were themselves largely material and earthbound. Hell, once a point of moral reference outside human experience, became a mere shorthand for the darkness within; and, with the disappearance of hell, came the loss of paradise, the final lapse into utopias that were now to be entirely of this world.

The missionaries who came to the New World in the sixteenth century brought a richer store, a blend of fifteen hundred years of Christendom allied to the new humanism of men like Erasmus and More. They still believed in the reality of a gospel kingdom. They were wrong, of course, and often wrongheaded, but they had an assurance in the face of tyranny that the twentieth century can hardly recognise.

In 1511 the Dominican friar Antonio de Montesinos denounced the European treatment of the New World Indians: 'You are all in a state of mortal sin,' he told the settlers, 'and you are going to live, and to die, in it, because of the cruelty and the tyranny you are inflicting on these innocent victims.' While in his *Utopia*, Thomas More ridiculed the material convictions that had reduced the civilised tribes of Europe to barbarism. His Utopians are full of wonder at the modern world:

> [They] wonder that any mortal takes pleasure in the uncertain sparkle of a tiny jewel or precious stone when he can look at a star or even the sun itself. They wonder that anyone can be so mad as to think himself more noble on account of the texture of a finer wool, since, however fine the texture is, a sheep once wore the wool and yet all the time was nothing more than a sheep.
>
> They wonder, too, that gold, which by its very nature is so useless, is now everywhere in the world valued so highly that man himself, through whose agency and for whose use it got this value, is priced much cheaper than gold itself . . .

On 14 November 1560, Ursúa's fleet left the Island of García. They came down through many abandoned villages whose inhabitants had fled on hearing of their imminent arrival. In one place they found signs of Orellana's passing, twenty years before: some Spanish hens, a horseshoe, and a white hat.

Their surviving brigantine foundered. Of the eleven ships which had left Topesana two months before, they now had only the two large barges, one of which was loaded with horses. Most of the men travelled rough, in one of the 200 canoes or on one of the surviving rafts. Those on the rafts had the hardest time, for they travelled slowest; and, since the fleet was on the move from dawn to dusk, they had to row constantly to keep up.

There was no shortage of wood to build new ships, or of cotton to caulk them; while the Indians had shown Orellana's men the value of a local pitch which they called *mene*: mixed with turtle grease, this was ideal for waterproofing. But Ursúa would not wait and they drifted on, huge, noisy, and cumbersome, the very picture of chaos and discontent.

Men had started to die of hunger or disease when, nine days after leaving the Island of García, the expedition arrived in the lands of the Machiparo. These covered a large area, to the east of the modern Brazilian frontier and upstream of the city of Manaus. The Indians here went naked, apart from a sort of loin-cloth. They built circular houses, with no walls, formed around a central pole, with a thatched roof that descended almost to the ground. Gonzalo de Zúñiga estimated that their lands stretched for over 500 miles.

At the first occupied village, the Indians received them with hostility. They had evacuated their women and children, and the Spanish found themselves facing between 300 and 400 armed warriors. Ursúa took no chances: he leapt on shore with a loaded harquebus in his left hand and an embroidered handkerchief in his right. The Indians, choosing to accept the token of peace rather than war, then offered to feed and house the expedition. All might have been well if Ursúa had been able to maintain discipline among his men. But the starving soldiers ran riot and began to strip the village of everything, so that many Indians took what they could and fled into the forest.

The Indians of Machiparo practised the farming of turtles and Custodio Hernández calls this the Village of the Turtles. They had more than 6,000 of them, each house having its own tanks. The Spanish now embarked on a wild fiesta, eating everything they could find. They made a vast communal turtle stew, they baked cakes and doughnuts, squandering 'with no thought for the future'. Worst of all, according to a scandalised Ortiguera, was that the mountain Indians from Peru, who were the servants of the expedition, wasted large quantities of maize, brewing beer and getting drunk.

The expedition rested here for thirty-three days, from 23 November until Christmas Day 1560. Ursúa's friends now realised that his life was in increasing danger. Soon there was not a turtle left in the village and, as the food supplies began to run out, many of the soldiers talked of abandoning their leader. But Ursúa's response to danger was never pragmatic. When his friends urged him to surround himself with a permanent bodyguard, he scorned the idea. He said he was in no need of protection when he was attended by 'so many men of Biscay', the Basque warriors of the north, all, as he supposed, his natural allies. Quixotically, he would say that one word in the Basque language would be enough to make all these men rise up and die for him.

Quixotic, too, was Ursúa's attitude to discipline. He identified some of the troublemakers in the camp, but he punished them by making them row in his lover's canoe. This was light in physical terms, but deeply humiliating. For a Spaniard to be seen in front of Indians and blacks, pressed into service like a galley slave, was an abomination. Many thought Ursúa had gone too far. Ortiguera was certainly right when he suggested it would have been better to have hanged the guilty men and be done; paradoxically, it would have caused less offence.

The image of Ursúa in his canoe, followed by doña Inés in hers, is a pleasing one: trailing wistfully down the Amazon, a sultry, Pre-Raphaelite vision of some medieval tale; they have eyes only for each other and remain oblivious of the Spaniards who sweat and strain at their paddles. The chroniclers do not name any of the rowers, but it's probable that men like Lope de Aguirre and Lorenzo de Zalduendo were among them, guilty men enslaved for a time by the most beautiful woman in Peru. They are described as overcome with lust, as, perhaps, they were – that would have been part of the humiliation after all.

But the lust for revenge soon began to run deeper and would have more lasting consequences.

Towards the end of December, Ursúa sent out a soldier named Pedro Alonso Galarza to explore one of the many tributaries in the vicinity of the village. He took a party of men in canoes and they soon found themselves in a huge lagoon which seemed to them to have no end. It was the rainy season, when the South American tropics are transformed into a series of overlapping freshwater seas. For the river-borne Indian, it was a time when half the continent became accessible, as the Amazon spread out into the Orinoco system to the north and, across the Gran Chaco, down to the Río de la Plata and the South Atlantic.

But the Spaniards hated this limitless expansion. Pedro Alonso and his men almost lost their lives, terrorised by the repetition of water and jungle, and they returned to camp after ten days. It was experiences like this which help to explain why the expedition was, in so many ways, so unadventurous. Once committed to the main stream of the Amazon, they did little but surrender to it, prisoners rather than explorers, passive in the face of a scale of things that surpassed everything they had ever known.

Once, when the Spaniards were there, the Machiparo were attacked by the Carari people from the Island of García. The two tribes were often at war and the invaders seem to have calculated that the presence of the Spaniards would make their old enemy vulnerable. They created a deep and colourful impression on the chroniclers as they came downriver to attack, 'playing their trumpets and flutes and other instruments of war'. But Ursúa chose to help the chief of the Machiparo and sent out fifty of his best harquebusiers under Juan de Vargas Zapata to fight on the Indian side. The resulting slaughter of the Carari was total.

It is here, among the Machiparo, that the name of Lope de Aguirre appears for the first time as one of the principal mutineers in the camp. The word the chroniclers use to describe him is *bullicioso*, which sums up two related aspects of his character: Aguirre is both 'rowdy' and 'restless'. All who knew him comment on how loud he was. He was the sort of man who would pick a quarrel in a bar for no reason and could be counted on to fight rough, without rules or honour. But even through the language of the harshest accounts, we can also see the shape of a man who was well able to think for himself, a man dissatisfied with life and unable to accept that he had not been destined for better things.

The rebellion against Pedro de Ursúa was to have been a small affair. At first, the rebels decided they would simply slip away in the night, with the two barges, and return to Peru. Aguirre seems to have convinced them of the futility of this enterprise and, as a result, the aim of the conspirators became the removal of Ursúa. Aguirre realised, perhaps now, perhaps much earlier, the extent to which Ursúa's unpopularity made him vulnerable. But he also knew that to exploit that vulnerability he needed an ally: preferably someone young, inexperienced, and manipulable from within Ursúa's inner circle. And so he began to work his gifts of flattery and deceit on don Fernando de Guzmán.

Don Fernando was young and aristocratic. He was vain; he was also from Seville, which, at the time, amounted to more or less the same thing. Seville was then the largest and most cosmopolitan city in Spain: '*Quien no ha visto Sevilla, no ha visto maravilla,*' ran the proverb ('He who has never seen Seville has never seen a marvel'). It was the great port for the Indies, rich, picturesque, and corrupt, the marketplace of the world, and it attracted adventurers from every part of Spain. Seville was the latest fashion in everything; while Aguirre and the Basques came out of the isolation of their mountains, the perfect symbol of the waning Middle Ages.

Aguirre chose well: don Fernando was a close friend of Ursúa and the coming treachery was completely unexpected. The betrayal, says Vázquez, would be the greatest the world had ever seen, 'on account of the deep and ancient friendship that he had for [Ursúa], which was such that the one would never eat without the other, and that often they would sleep together, even though each had his own bed . . .'

The expedition lingered in the Village of the Turtles until all supplies were exhausted. They spent Chritmas Day there and, on the following day, they departed. They travelled through a familiar landscape of deserted villages until, on 27 December, they stopped at a place which Custodio Hernández calls Mozomoco, but which was so insignificant that none of the other chroniclers can remember its name. This patch of mud and water was to be the terminus of Ursúa's Amazonian adventure.

There were several portents in the days before Ursúa's death. One of his friends, out for an evening stroll, saw a ghost passing by Ursúa's hut which murmured, 'Pedro de Ursúa, governor of El Dorado and Omagua, may God pardon you.' All the chroniclers assure us there can be no doubt about this. While a few hours before Ursúa died, Pedro Portillo, the priest from Moyobamba who had been so miserably abused, made a last appearance. Dying of illness and hunger, he cursed Ursúa for having made him come on the expedition and begged for food. When Ursúa told him he had none to give, Portillo raised his arms, saying: 'May justice from heaven – since there is none in this world – come upon him who has so cruelly used me.'

The conspirators chose New Year's Eve to murder Ursúa. They gathered around don Fernando. He had finally been convinced of the need to act, though the chroniclers are unsure about the extent of his enthusiasm. Lope de Aguirre made a brief speech: the problem, he said, was that the expedition had set out to discover new lands and that Ursúa had shown himself incapable of leadership. After all the sacrifices, the hunger and sickness and disappointment, it was only just that Ursúa should die. The people, said Aguirre, have become 'sad, disconsolate, and full of grief'. So, he concluded, 'let us not now leave this affair to others, for we do not know what may come of it.'

At three o'clock in the morning of New Year's Day 1561, they left for Ursúa's hut. They found him in his hammock, perhaps alone, or with a friend, or attended by his servants, no one agrees. There were thirteen conspirators in all, including Lope de Aguirre, the 'fountain and creator of all evil', as Vázquez puts it.

Caesar-like, Ursúa confronted the treachery of his closest friend and in a moment was hacked to death. His murderers ran shrieking through the camp: 'Long live the king, for the tyrant is dead!' Then they found the loyal Juan de Vargas Zapata, who had defended Ursúa from criticism all the way down the river. He, too, was hacked to pieces and the cry now was: 'Freedom, freedom, long live the king!'

Such was the death of Pedro de Ursúa, the *caballero* from Navarre. He was about thirty-five years old, a great horseman, graceful in speech, 'more inclined to mercy than to justice', says Vázquez; much given to women, though never boastful of his conquests. With many abilities, according to most of those who knew him; and yet, clearly flawed: 'As it is said that few mortals are free from fault, so among [his] virtues he had a number of vices and bad habits – though it was said that his lover, doña Inés, was responsible for most of them . . .' And Vázquez completes the portrait: Ursúa was somewhat covetous; ungrateful at times to friends, uncharitable towards the sick and needy, slow to forgive or forget.

Though we cannot trust the chroniclers very far in matters of judgment, this is a human catalogue and a plausible one. None of the eye-witnesses regarded Ursúa's death as a tragedy in personal terms. The warmth which they express for him is all in the past, from a time when he was fond of his men, affable and approachable. That side of his character had vanished on the Amazon, so much so, says Vázquez, that 'those of us who had known him from the beginning used to say to each other that it wasn't possible this could be Pedro de Ursúa.'

Perhaps Ursúa simply gave up the struggle, through illness or some other cause. He took wild risks with his life towards the end, refused all advice, ignored his friends. But it is more likely that he suffered from presumption, a feeling that he had survived this kind of life for so long that he would never die from it. Perhaps doña Inés encouraged his sense of being invulnerable, perhaps life with her was simply more fun than this endless descent of a river whose promise was always unfulfilled. His death was violent, but strangely casual, as if it were the conclusion to something that had already ended a long time before.

At dawn on New Year's Day, doña Inés requested permission to bury the dead. Don Fernando ordered Ursúa's slaves to dig a pit and the commander of the fleet was placed side by side with Juan de Vargas, for, 'as they had been such good friends in life', said don Fernando, 'it was not right to separate them in death.'

Don Fernando was proclaimed general, with Lope de Aguirre as his *maestre de campo*, or second-in-command. The men then proceeded to elect further officers, under a sudden impulse of democracy. Indeed, says Ortiguera haughtily, 'they appointed more . . . officers than there were soldiers in the camp'. To round off the day, they took out the sacramental wine and drank until not a drop was left.

Don Fernando, however, was troubled by what he had done and decided to try to legalise his position. A long document was drawn up, setting out the justification for the murder of the viceroy's appointed leader. Don Fernando signed it first, then passed it to his second-in-command. And now, suddenly, with that mixture of arrogance and theatricality for which he will become famous, Lope de Aguirre appears, takes the document, and signs: 'Lope de Aguirre, traitor.'

He showed it to those around him and then began a remarkable speech:

> What madness, what foolishness is this that has overcome you all? That having killed the king's governor, one who was clothed with royal powers . . . and who represented his royal person, you should now think of excusing yourselves from guilt? All who have played a part have been traitors. And even if we were now to discover and settle a new land, and even if it were to be better than Peru itself, the first *bachiller* to come along would cut off our heads. Anyone who thinks otherwise has lost all reason . . .

Now, for the first time, we hear Aguirre's voice at length. Foreshadowed all the way from Cuzco, the traitor of El Dorado finally intervenes. He is lucid and says calmly what needs to be said. The murder of Ursúa, he tells the men, is either an act of butchery on the part of a band of disgruntled adventurers; or it is a symbolic act of rebellion against the crown of Spain. If they did not now lay claim to the second of these images, they would surely find themselves judged in terms of the first.

When they reflected in the light of day, most of the soldiers seem to have believed that their best option was to carry on with the expedition, in the hope of some sensational discovery that might make the crown more lenient towards them. But Aguirre understood the futility of such an approach. He saw there was no way the murder of Ursúa could be legitimated in the eyes of the old order. Even if they went on to discover a new Peru, they would still die as common criminals. They had crossed boundaries that could never be crossed without the world ceasing to be what it had been. Now he asked them to acknowledge the immensity of what they had done, rather than dabble in legal pretence, in the vain hope that they could minimise it.

The challenge before them was to become the kind of men their actions already supposed them to be: independent and self-creating. It was an idea that would carry Aguirre a long way; so far, that, a few months later, in another anonymous village on the Amazon, he was to make a speech which some historians have taken as the first declaration of an independent America.

Lope de Aguirre seems always to have been fascinated by the idea of the traitor. It was part of his search for self-definition and it appealed to his love of drama. To acknowledge oneself a traitor was to achieve recognition in the face of the established world: no one would remember Judas if he hadn't betrayed Christ. But it was also to play with that world, to lay bare the arbitrary rules and petty restrictions by which it functioned. And it opened the way, far into the future, for the rewriting of the rules themselves, at that moment of transition when the traitor to the crown slips into the new role as the hero of national independence.

Always, at the back of his mind, Aguirre had the example of another great Peruvian traitor, Gonzalo Pizarro. Gonzalo had become a legend in the early 1540s, when he emerged from the jungle in rags after the failure of his Amazonian expedition. He had gone on to seize the government of Peru and to rule the country from 1544 until 1548. During those four years the colony paid nothing to the national treasury in Spain. Gonzalo shared with his brother Francisco the belief that Peru belonged to those who had conquered it, rather than to the crown which threatened to grow fat on its revenues; and in this attitude he would be followed by Aguirre.

What Aguirre never forgot, however, was that Gonzalo Pizarro had been defeated, not by military, but by diplomatic means. Gonzalo had a brilliant military strategist as his *maestre de campo*: Francisco de Carvajal, known as the 'demon of the Andes', a pathological killer who shared some of Aguirre's characteristics. But all of Carvajal's skills were useless beside the diplomatic campaign launched by the Spanish crown. Licenciado Pedro de la Gasca was sent to Peru as a royal emissary in 1547, to put down Gonzalo's rebellion. When the eventual confrontation on the battlefield came in 1548, outside Cuzco, it was purely symbolic. Gonzalo had already been fatally undermined. There was a minor skirmish and then virtually all the rebellious forces went over to the royalist side. Gonzalo was executed the following day.

Pedro de la Gasca was a *licenciado* ('licentiate'), one of the *letrados*, the band of lawyers who followed in the train of the Conquest and whom Aguirre hated more than anyone. In his eyes, they were the men who were trained in the traditional rules and whose only function in life was to manipulate them on behalf of the powerful. This explains the scornful tone of his speech when he says: 'The first *bachiller* to come along would cut off our heads.' For the *bachiller*, too, is a *letrado*, one immediately below the *licenciado* in rank.

In all official writings, Gonzalo Pizarro is the complete traitor; but Aguirre remembers the popular warrior-leader brought down by the pettiness of officialdom and the treachery of friends. From Gonzalo's story Aguirre takes three things: a certain fatalism in the face of history, a belief that no one can be trusted, and the knowledge that absolute power is one of life's most beguiling and dangerous fictions.

El Dorado, too, he finally accepted, was a fiction, and a dishonourable one. Or, if it had any meaning, it was only in the past. '*Qué buena tierra era el Perú*', he reminded the men, who were now, increasingly, *his* men. Peru had been the real El Dorado of the New World. The earliest *conquistadores* had found riches beyond imagining. But for those who had come too late and missed the chance of a lifetime, there could be hope only in struggle. Aguirre knew he had a fighting force of great experience and effectiveness, if only he could unify and discipline it. So now he began to develop a strategy to get the expedition back to Peru, where they could all take their chances: 'Let us sell our lives', he concluded, 'before we are forced to give them away.'

# SEVEN

SUDDENLY, ALMOST WITHOUT warning, Peru vanishes into Brazil. Once, this tangle of heat and light flowed on, indivisible, through the country of the Omagua. But the Treaty of Madrid in 1750 confirmed Tabatinga as the crossing point between two empires, a division of the spoils that left almost half of South America to the Portuguese.

The language changes, still familiar, but now incomprehensible, a stream of half-recognised words that add up to nothing. If you can read Spanish then you can read Portuguese, but there communication ends. Routine travellers' questions of 'how much?' or 'how far?' suddenly bring unexpected challenges. The world shrinks, becomes almost entirely literary. We sat on the waterfront, watching the boats on the river, and read everything around us, the public notices, scraps of old Brazilian newspapers, a torn leaf from a child's school-book. Later, things will improve, but, for now, this anonymity, the heat and flies in a country where you have lost your voice, is dispiriting.

There are some places in the world you only remember because it was hot there. The dry heat of a desert town, where the wind burns the skin and you long for the unmoving air of late afternoon. Joyful places, where the heat brings people on to the streets in celebration. The sad heat of small towns, where everyone retreats behind shuttered windows and, for the traveller, there's only the loneliness of the empty streets, where not even a stray cat crosses the line between sun and shadow.

From Iquitos we had passed downriver without difficulty.

Beyond the Brazilian frontier at Tabatinga it became even easier. Sometimes it hardly felt like travelling at all. You only noticed the noise of the engines when the boat slowed and stopped at some landing stage that was no different from the one before or the one to come.

The play of light on green forest and yellow water is monotonous. The sky is held between white and grey. It rains much of the time and there's almost no one to talk to. Those who can afford it go by plane. But there was an eccentric official of the World Bank, going home the long way to Philadelphia, and a woman from Mexico who for a week wore the same sweat shirt, or maybe she had more than one, saying 'Alaska is the way America was'.

Often the boat changed course to pass shoals of logs being towed downstream. Many of them were so heavy that they would have sunk if they'd come adrift. A man sat motionless among them, sometimes wandering up and down to check the fastenings, apparently walking on water.

In the evenings, the light fades quickly over the roof of the forest. In the afterglow, strange forms appear in silhouette. Dying men raise their arms in desperation towards the sky or hang from gallows in mute crucifixion. The heat subsides and the steady rain feels cool against clothes sodden with the perspiration of the day.

In the Middle Ages, people believed that all the great rivers of the world flowed out of Paradise. They told a story of Adam who, when he was old and sick, asked his son Seth to find a way back up river, to beg for oil from the Tree of Mercy, so that he might not die. But when Seth reached Paradise the gates were closed and the angel would not let him enter.

Today the river is sick, sweats out the rubbish and diseases of a continent. After the great cholera epidemic of 1991 devastated the Peruvian coast, it soon swept down the Amazon, and by April it had reached Tabatinga. Peruvians found themselves the pariahs of South America, living out what one Peruvian writer called 'a sort of Spielberg in reverse', as the country rushed headlong into a past that had once seemed unalterably remote.

The land of Brazil is named after the brazilwood that grows there. This is a fact, though it sometimes seems an improbable one, as if the relationship should have been the other way round. Europeans discovered the country at the very start of the sixteenth century, and Amerigo Vespucci, the man who unwittingly gave his name to America, was soon chronicling an exploration along 2,000 miles of its coastline. In 1535, the Portuguese sailed up the Amazon from the Atlantic and may have reached as far as the mouth of the Negro, seven years before Francisco de Orellana and his men descended from the west.

But in those days nobody cared much about Brazil. First impressions suggested that it was an island, vast and impoverished, with no future, except, of course, for the brazilwood and the possibility that, if it really was an island, there might be a way round it to the spice islands of the East Indies. It was an unheroic beginning, but the natives were unfriendly and disposed to cannibalism, and there were none of the attractions of the settled societies of Mexico or Peru.


Don Fernando and his men moved out of the village where Ursúa had been murdered on 7 January 1561. They abandoned one of their two surviving barges, leaving it to rot behind them, and travelled on with a cargo of dying horses in the other. '[And so] we left this place of our undoing', says one of the chroniclers, 'and came to another village that would be about twenty leagues [about 70 miles] down stream.'

This new village, as empty as all the rest, they called the Village of the Brigantines. It lay between 200 and 300 miles upstream of modern Manaus, and here they spent eighty-one days rebuilding the fleet. Don Fernando set the specialist boatbuilders to work: four Spanish overseers and the twenty black slaves who were the carpenters of the expedition. They were to make two new brigantines which would take them out into the Atlantic, on the first stage of their journey back to Peru.

The village was a wretched place for so long a stay. There was almost nothing to eat, apart from manioc. Most of this was of the bitter variety which contains lethal doses of prussic acid. It can be safely eaten, but first it must be processed. Some of the highland Indians, through desperation or lack of knowledge, ate it raw and died miserably. The Spanish disembarked the surviving horses and butchered them, so that in death, at least, they might find a role denied to them in life. When they had eaten all the horses, they ate the dogs, and finally were reduced to eating turkey vultures, dark birds with grotesque bare red heads, no doubt as revolting a prospect then as now. And all the time they were savaged by mosquitoes.

In the Village of the Brigantines, Aguirre embarked on a series of killings that would continue until the end of his life. The chroniclers talk of them as if they were completely random. With time they would become so, but in the beginning they did have an order and a motive. Keeping control in remote places traditionally depended on two things: the actual power of a leader to command obedience through his physical strength or force of personality; and his symbolic power, as one who connected everyone on the expedition with the royal system of justice they had left behind.

Of these two functions, the second was probably the more significant. The *gobernador* was the visual embodiment of an abstraction that must otherwise have seemed increasingly unreal in unfamiliar surroundings. But now the legitimate *gobernador* was dead and all symbolic bonds had been broken. Power now lay with anyone who could seize and defend it, and the apparent irrationality of Aguirre's reign of terror begins to acquire its own logic.

The first man to die was García de Arce, the finest harquebusier on the expedition. This alone might have been reason for his murder, but he had also been close to Ursúa, and suspicion fell on him because he had already shown himself to be an independent commander when he abandoned Juan de Vargas on the Huallaga river. García de Arce was leaning against a tree, watching the boat-builders at work, when Aguirre came up to him with a group of his men, including a Portuguese shoemaker called Anton Llamoso or Llamaso. Llamoso was one of the true sadists in the camp, a man Aguirre was to use several times for the sort of killings others would not contemplate. In a moment, García de Arce was nailed to the tree by a weapon made from a long shoemaker's needle. Aguirre then had him hanged with a notice tied across his chest that read: 'For services to king and governor.'

There were half-a-dozen more killings in the days to come. The men died in different ways; stabbed, shot, or garrotted. There seems to have been no pattern, except that death by garrotting was, by its nature, more formal, more ritualised, closer to execution than assassination, often used as a public means to impress or deter.

Garrotting, as the preferred method of execution, continued in Spain until very recent times. In its modern form, an iron collar was placed around the victim's neck; the collar was then tightened until death occurred by asphyxiation or dislocation of the spinal column. A British military observer in 1837 enthused: 'I have no hesitation in pronouncing death by the garrot, at once the most manly and the least offensive to the eye.' Whether the sixteenth-century method was as pleasing to the eye is not so sure. The chroniclers never talk about the detail of such things, they were commonplace. The victim was usually seated in a chair fixed to a post; a cord was tied around the neck, and then a stick – the original sense of *garrot* is 'packing-stick' – was inserted between the cord and neck and twisted until the victim was strangled.

One of the men killed at this time, Christóbal Hernández, took a miraculously long time to die. He was 'given death by a thousand forms', says Gonzalo de Zúñiga; he was set upon with spear and dagger, knife and stones, 'and they could not . . . [even] wound him, for he must have been in possession of some relics [which protected him].' In the end, he drowned in the Amazon, while a team of harquebusiers fired on him from the bank.

Aguirre then killed Pedro Hernández, the expedition's paymaster; and a *mestizo*, Pedro de Miranda. They were hanged from a tree, with a sign saying '*Por amotinadorcillos*' ('for being dirty little traitors') about their necks. But as Aguirre struggled to impose order through terror, he inevitably met with resistance. Don Fernando, who was to spend the rest of his short life contemplating the slow unravelling of his always nominal power, occasionally tried to assert himself. At one point he took the decision to remove Aguirre as his *maestre de campo* and to give the job to another man, Juan Alonso de la Bandera. It was a foolish, probably desperate, move that would seal his own fate and that of all those who were close to him.

The camp now waited to see what Aguirre would do. Rumours were the stuff of everyday life, a problem Aguirre was soon to deal with by proclaiming that nobody could talk to anyone else in private, on pain of death. The expedition's canoes began to vanish and, after a time, of the more than 150 they had brought to the village only twenty largely unserviceable ones remained. Some said the Indians were stealing them, but others guessed that Aguirre was secretly casting them off by night to block all means of escape.

Spaniards venturing into the jungle in search of food were attacked and killed by Indians. The chroniclers mention Sebastián Gómez, captain of the sea, a man named Molina, Villarreal, Pedro Díaz, Anton Rodríguez, a Mendoza, a Castro, all of whom died in this way. Pedro de Monguía says that four of the Spaniards were cooked and eaten. This is not very likely, but no doubt people believed it and Monguía himself is keen to assure us it was so; for they went and looked for their comrades, he says, and found traces of their cooked flesh, and they saw the Indians dressed in their clothes.

The heat was so intense that many of the Spaniards took to going naked. Everyone suffered from a lack of salt in their diet. They foraged for jungle fruits, pineapples and *chatos*, 'which are like oranges, only white'. There was security nowhere. The jungle was dangerous and the camp always uncertain, 'for, as the refrain goes', noted Ortiguera, 'the man who is loyal will only live as long as the traitor decides.' Only Aguirre seemed to see the situation as a challenge. In his struggle with Juan Alonso de la Bandera, he showed himself in every way the more cunning and the more intelligent. Always on the alert, he never slept in his own hut, and, while others took off their clothes, he kept to his armour. He was friendly to the men, coaxing, almost playful. Above all, he relied on his Basque comrades for protection: 'They were all Basques [in his bodyguard]', lamented Gonzalo de Zúñiga; 'sailors and men from the coast, of little honour . . . a most wicked and accursed people.'

Juan Alonso very soon brought about his own undoing. As *maestre de campo* he grew proud and overbearing. Most foolish of all, he planned to seize the sexual prize of the expedition, Ursúa's former lover, the beautiful doña Inés. After Ursúa's death, she had become the lover of Lorenzo de Zalduendo, Ursúa's old recruiting agent in Cuzco. In social terms this was a great descent, but, whatever her feelings may have been, Zalduendo must have seemed a good choice. She knew him, at least. He was the captain of don Fernando's personal bodyguard, resourceful and apparently well able to take care of himself and her.

Aguirre and Zalduendo conspired to have Juan Alonso murdered. On 16 February 1561, he was shot down during a game of cards and Aguirre was once again *maestre de campo*.

But more important than the long list of killings was the political activity that occupied the spaces in between. It is this alone that gives to Aguirre's character an interest beyond that of the common tyrant or the mercenary assassin.

He organised three general meetings for three different purposes. Each involved a speech. At the first two meetings don Fernando addressed the men, but on the last occasion it was Aguirre himself. This was the moment when he called on his soldiers to renounce their origins and to begin again, as citizens of a New World. After each speech the men were asked to state their opinions and to sign a document pledging themselves to work for a common future. It's easy to see that much of this was mere play, a classic tactic that gave Aguirre the chance to see who stood where and to prepare for the elimination of those who were in his way. But there was more to it.

In advance of the first meeting, Aguirre persuaded don Fernando to resign his position as general and commander of the fleet and, in effect, to offer himself for re-election before the men. One of the priests said mass and afterwards all gathered in the open in front of don Fernando's hut. He ceremonially took a halberd in his hands and told the men he wanted them to be free to make whatever choice they wished as to who should lead them. Then he thrust the halberd into the ground as a symbol of the renunciation of power. Most of the men seemed to have been impressed by the gesture. They made it clear that they wanted to continue with don Fernando. A document was drawn up and signed by nearly everyone.

Then, in the presence of the priest, there was a great swearing of oaths. The chroniclers make much of this ritual. The oaths, they say, were so powerful that anyone who broke them would be liable to excommunication, placed so far beyond hope of salvation 'that he could not be absolved, save only by the Supreme Pontiff himself'.

On the second occasion, don Fernando offered the men a choice of whether they wished to continue with the expedition or return to Peru. Aguirre and his followers said that they were all for returning. The men would grow old on this river before they found anything. Peru meant land, horses, beautiful women, riches in gold and silver. Above all, in Peru they would find comrades who would join them in the fight for what was theirs.

Aguirre's message won the day. Everyone, through desire or fear or lack of alternatives, agreed to go back to Peru. All signed their intention and then they dispersed.

The third meeting was a much more significant affair. It was here that Aguirre spoke for the first time in public of the need to break all ties with Spain. He introduced the subject almost casually. 'Before we can return to Peru', he said, 'there are one or two formalities (*una ó dos diligencias*) to attend to.' The first of these, he went on, 'is that we should denaturalise ourselves from Spain' (*que nos desnaturemos de España*); 'that we should profess and acknowledge that the king [of Spain], don Felipe, is not our king, nor our natural lord, and that we should deny him vassal-age.'

Aguirre is certainly not the first Spaniard to talk of denaturalisation, of giving up one's nationality, as we would say. The verb *desnaturar* exists in Spanish from the thirteenth century and its meaning is clear: it is the action of the vassal who breaks the bonds that tie him to his liege lord. In fourteenth-century Castile, a formal procedure was available by which members of the high nobility could 'denaturalise' themselves from king and country, and the idea was understood in other European countries also.

So, for some historians, Aguirre's speech on the Amazon is simply a return to the politics of the past, to the closed, intimate world that the Spanish call *la patria chica*, the little country, in opposition to the ever-expanding world of the Spanish empire. For others, on the contrary, Aguirre is one of the first of the new Americans, looking forward to an independence that will one day be the goal of all those to whom the mother country has nothing left to give.

But perhaps this clash of past and future, regressive and progressive, is too simple. It sees the development of the nation state as Europe's natural destiny, where it was, perhaps, only an historical diversion. In many places the process of 'naturalisation' was slow – and in Spain it was never completed. Today, in the strongholds of Basque separatism, along the coast of Guipúzcoa or in Vitoria in Alava, one of the commonest slogans on the walls is: 'The Basque country has no king.' The Amazonian voice of the unassimilated is still adrift, without a home in time or space.

The Basques were never fully enclosed in the world of empire. They kept their language, unrelated to any other, older than Greek, older than the oldest languages of Europe. And when, in the early modern period, their historians came to re-write the story of their culture, they reached out far beyond the boundaries of the nation state. They claimed that the Basques descended from Tubal, one of the grandsons of Noah. Their rights, they said, belonged to the origins of the world itself and were grounded in natural law, millennia before the coming of the Spanish. All Basques were equal, all were *hidalgos*, for they had never accepted political domination; and if they made contributions to the Spanish treasury, it was in the form of gifts, not tribute, for the king of Spain was never lord over the Basque lands.

Once we have ceased to be Spanish, Aguirre told his men, we should elect don Fernando to be our 'prince, lord, and rightful king, so that we may crown him in Peru, when we arrive there'. Aguirre, as *maestre de campo*, then went forward to kiss don Fernando's hand. All the captains followed, with the rest of the men after. Don Fernando was open-mouthed. The chroniclers talk of his reactions in different ways and it's obvious that they had difficulty working them out. But, even with his youth and inexperience, it must have occurred to him that the higher he was promoted, the further he was from power, and the more vulnerable.

Nevertheless, from that time on, don Fernando decided to behave like a king. Perhaps he thought it was the safest thing for him to do. He began to eat alone and was served with as much regal show as the camp could manage. He became grave and haughty, and he took to prefacing his letters and written orders with the words: 'Don Fernando de Guzmán, by the Grace of God prince of Tierra Firme [the Spanish Main] and of Peru and of the Kingdom of Chile.' His royal presence was formally announced by the blowing of trumpets and the beating of drums. But it was to be a brief and unmemorable reign, and two months later he was dead.

On 30 March 1561, the expedition set off again with two new brigantines. One was named *Victory*, under the command of don Fernando, the other *Santiago*, under Aguirre. The plan was to sail as quickly as possible to the nearest Spanish settlement that could be reached in the direction of the river's flow. This was the island of Margarita, off the Venezuelan coast, to the west of Trinidad. It was several thousand miles away, but they probably had an idea of the distance, since Orellana and his men had made a landfall on the island of Cubagua, only a few miles from Margarita, at the end of their own journey down the Amazon in 1542.

Aguirre's plan was to move on quickly from Margarita, after re-supplying the expedition, and to sail westwards to the Panamanian Isthmus before the authorities had news of their coming. They would sack the principal town of Nombre de Dios, cross over to the Pacific coast of the Isthmus, seize the Panamanian fleet, and descend on Peru. The shortage in their numbers would be made up by supporters who would join them in Panama and by the hundreds of black slaves they proposed to recruit with offers of freedom. It was never likely that this desperate plan would come to anything, and Aguirre seems to have been less and less sure as the expedition moved on. The journey from the Village of the Brigantines to Margarita Island took nearly four months and the experience was enough to test Aguirre's resolution to the point where he seems finally to have lost his reason.

There has never been absolute certainty about the route the expedition followed in order to reach Margarita Island. Most modern historians believe that Aguirre took the obvious way, in the path of Orellana, going straight down the Amazon to its mouth, then turning north-west for the long sea-journey up the coast. But there has always been a suspicion that he found an alternative route, one which would have taken the fleet out of the Amazon basin and into the Orinoco river-system. According to this theory, he would have discovered the Casiquiare Canal, a natural river link that generally flows from the Upper Orinoco south-west into the Río Negro, though occasionally in the reverse direction, and which otherwise remained unknown to the Europeans until 1744. Aguirre would have descended the Orinoco, entering the Atlantic to the south-east of Trinidad.

The speculation derives mainly from a passage in the chronicle of Francisco Vázquez. He is a shrewd observer in many ways and he states explicitly that, some time after leaving the

Village of the Brigantines, the fleet changed course. Where previously they had been running with the stream along the right bank of the Amazon, they now took a branch of the river which led off to the left. Aguirre made the decision, Vázquez says, because he had news that further down the Amazon they would come to rich land and he feared the men would wish to stay there, rather than follow him back to Peru.

It's just possible that they entered some river like the Japurá, but little of what the chroniclers have to say later would correspond to such a journey, and it seems unlikely that they ever left the main stream of the Amazon. Nevertheless, another eyewitness, Custodio Hernández, tells another version of the same story, and the question will never be finally resolved. Perhaps the answer is a simple one: that they lost their way among islands in the ever-widening river and that the general atmosphere of suspicion in the fleet led to the sort of stories we find reflected in the chronicles.

On Maundy Thursday, 3 April 1561, they reached an Indian village at dawn and Aguirre decided to spend Easter there. Vázquez calls it a place 'of few houses and many mosquitoes'. Much of the land was flooded. For the first time they saw houses that were thatched with straw, suggesting the proximity of open grass lands. They found a little maize and did some fishing, and, after a while, naked Indians came to trade with them.

On Easter Monday they travelled on and, the next day, came to a large village, one of the most seductive places they ever found on the Amazon. It stretched for seven miles along the river bank, confined by a lagoon on the other side, so that it occupied, the chroniclers say, a strip of land no wider than a crossbow shot might reach. The Indians here were confident, well disposed towards the intruders; and they traded 'with such friendship as if they had been dealing with [the Spanish] all their lives'.

After the deprivation of the previous weeks, this was paradise. There were turkeys, duck, and tapirs, fish, turtles, wild pig, manatees, yams and pumpkins. The Indians made a kind of red wine, from maize, yucca, and sugar, that they fermented in large earthen jars, 'like the wine of Castile'. The Indians were also, according to Vázquez, *subtilísimos ladrones* ('the most artful of thieves'), taking clothes, arms, and anything else they could find while the Spaniards were asleep. But even this failed to disturb the atmosphere. The Spanish murdered some of the Indians as a warning, but 'they [did not] make much ado' about it and continued to trade peaceably, as before.

The Spanish settled in for a long stay and were to remain from 8 April until 25 May. Don Fernando took up residence in one section of the village with his retinue. Lope de Aguirre and his closest associates occupied the strategically important middle section, close to the brigantines, with the rest of the men on the other side. This meant that don Fernando could only communicate with the men, or they with him, by crossing the lines held by Aguirre. The village lay between the river Purús and the Negro, a little upstream of Manaus.

It was to be the setting for a series of killings that seemed so intense, so out of the ordinary, even in so extraordinary a world as they had now lived in for many months, that they called the village the Pueblo de la Matanza (Village of the Massacre).

There is every likelihood that it was don Fernando, rather than Aguirre, who brought on the immediate crisis. He called a council of his advisers from which Aguirre was ostentatiously excluded. Don Fernando clearly understood that he was unlikely to live long unless he could deal with Aguirre in some way, but he oscillated fatally between a desire for conciliation and the necessity for violent action. This uncertainty played into Aguirre's hands. Under threat, he now had the motive for removing don Fernando. But, before that, he would remove some of the lesser challengers.

The first to die here was Lorenzo de Zalduendo. He had ordered some mattresses to be sent on board one of the brigantines, so that doña Inés and her entourage could travel more comfortably. Whether out of jealousy, as some say, or for other reasons, Aguirre refused to allow this. He sent the mattresses back, saying there was no room for such things. Zalduendo correctly saw this as a sentence of death and took refuge in don

Fernando's quarters. But Aguirre followed him in rage and stabbed him repeatedly until he died. All the while, don Fernando looked on, watching, as he must have realised, the rehearsal for his own imminent extinction.

With Zalduendo dead and don Fernando unable to act, doña Inés was now in a hopeless position. Aguirre called for the Portuguese shoemaker, Llamoso, and a *mestizo*, Francisco de Carrión. Llamoso, 'the most cruel, most fiendish traitor men have ever seen, the minister of Satan', led the way. They refused doña Inés even the time for confession; one held her down by the hair, the other stabbed her.

Finally the murderers took her keys and stole her jewels and everything that she had. The chroniclers linger over the details, how she drowned in her own blood on the floor of the hut, undefended now even by her extraordinary beauty. They try to understand the depths of such sadism, 'for certainly few men would have had the heart to kill a woman as beautiful as she'. Even the most misogynistic of the chroniclers, those outraged by her private life and the 'evil ways she had continued in since she left Peru' – even they manage to convey a feeling of pity at the deed. They took her life, says one, 'in such a barbarous manner that, after her death, even the most hardened men in the camp were broken-hearted at the sight of the mangled victim, for this was the most cruel act that had been perpetrated'.

But, of course, it could not end there. Aguirre now took to playing with don Fernando. He abused him openly in front of everyone, saying that, after all, you could never trust a *sevillano*; and so don Fernando, native of Seville, quietly surrendered. 'It seemed that he carried death in his eyes,' and had become 'so timid and listless that for the care of his own life he took but little note'.

The massacre was prepared during the night of 21 May. Aguirre divided his men into groups of ten to a dozen. Each squad was given the name of a victim. Don Fernando's death, however, was entrusted to two men only, Martín Pérez and Juan de Aguirre, and the order was known to no one else, for even in the present state of the camp there were many who would hesitate before the murder of a king.

153

They kept watch until dawn, fearing that in a night attack they ran the risk of killing the wrong person, even of killing each other. Aguirre positioned them by the ships, so that none of the victims would have a chance to escape. Alonso de Montoya and Miguel Bovedo, two close friends of don Fernando, were the first to die. Then Aguirre himself struck down a priest, Alonso Henao; he found him asleep on a mattress and staked him to the ground with his sword.

They arrived at don Fernando's hut. He received them in his nightshirt, saying to Aguirre: 'What is this, *padre mío*?', as if the end could have been in doubt. They killed Miguel Serrano de Cáceres, Gonzalo Duarte, and Baltasar Toscano; and then, when the other men had gone, don Fernando, almost in secret, lost his life to two shots from a harquebus.

He was young – only about twenty-five years old – of medium height and a quiet disposition, say the chroniclers. No doubt a younger son with no future in Spain who came to the New World in search of something better, only to find himself caught up in a horror he could not hope to understand. None of the chroniclers can excuse his role in the murder of Ursúa, though some speak more in sorrow than in anger: 'And may it please God', says Ortiguera, 'to have granted him true contrition, so that his soul might not be lost by cause of that same infamy which made him lose his life.' Vázquez, as he often does, adds a homely detail to the rather bland generalisations of the other chroniclers: don Fernando, he says, 'was dissolute and gluttonous; a lover of eating and drinking, especially fruits and doughnuts (*buñuelos*) and cakes, in search of which he was ever vigilant; and whosoever wished to be his friend could, by means of any of these, easily win him over'.

The camp now settled into the peace of exhaustion. Aguirre called a meeting, surrounded by a bodyguard of eighty handpicked soldiers. What had happened, he said, was natural, inevitable, in time of war. Don Fernando and his captains knew nothing of leadership and so they had been marked to die. From here on, he, Aguirre, would command and there would be order. Henceforth, there would be no private discussions, only

154

silence and action. All this, he declared, in the name of Lope de Aguirre, the Wrath of God, Prince of Freedom and of the Kingdom of Tierra Firme and the Provinces of Chile, Lord of all South America, from the Isthmus of Panama to the Strait of Magellan, 'where . . . the wide North Sea . . . joins that other Sea which men call the Southern': lord of all that had been discovered and of all that remained to be discovered.

Now, at last, Aguirre could play on an empty stage of his own choosing. The tiny, enclosed world of an Amazonian village would serve for the great roles buried in his imagination. Aguirre would never lose his love of the theatrical, even in the final moments of his life. But he never fell victim to it either. He knew how much of power depended on the illusion of power. This helps to explain his constant insecurity and his viciousness. For him, becoming a leader was like moving into a large rambling house with uncountable rooms. You could never know the extent of your domain and you could never hope to be everywhere at once. What lay in those rooms which you had never seen, perhaps would never see, brought a fascination that was sometimes close to terror.

But if Aguirre looked back fondly to an old world of primitive fear, he also looked forward, towards a new, less mythic world. If he was the Wrath of God, he was also Prince of Freedom. Even now, he wanted to say, it was possible to begin again: to claim that world in which reward went with merit, success with hard work, and victory to the man who knew who he was and had the courage to act on it.

Aguirre reorganised the command structure of the expedition. He made Martín Pérez his *maestre de campo*. He elevated shipwrights and carpenters; and he demoted the only surviving man of high social status, the *comendador* Juan de Guevara, promising him in return a pension of 20,000 gold *pesos*, to be paid once they reached Tierra Firme. And so order was restored for a time and the fleet moved on in silence.

On a sweltering evening in early September we began to see the lights of a great city, by far the largest place we had seen since leaving Iquitos. Manaus, the capital of the State of Amazonas, is 900 miles from Tabatinga. Three hours by air from Lima, four from Rio, five from Miami, it's a very long journey by boat. The city lies at the confluence of the Río Negro and the Solimões and marks the point at which the Brazilian Amazon begins.

It's been called Manaus only since the middle of the nineteenth century. As late as 1870, it was just a village of 5,000 people, the natural descendant of the seventeenth-century fortress which the Portuguese placed to guard their interests at the mouth of the Negro. Then came a brief moment of fame, so unlikely and so fleeting that romance still clings to the name of Manaus. From 1880 to 1910 almost all the rubber consumed in the world passed through here. Manaus became one of the richest places on earth, as the large merchant houses prospered at the apex of a credit system designed to keep all those below in an endlessly repeating cycle of debt.

Here the rubber-tappers bought their supplies, their simple tools and overpriced food, before setting off into the green hell which would never make their fortunes. While those who stayed behind in Manaus tried to turn their city into one of the wonders of the world. In many ways they succeeded, and the greatest symbol of their triumph remains the wide, extravagant building which in English is called the Opera House.

The Teatro Amazonas, which is its Portuguese name, was inaugurated in 1896, at the very height of the rubber boom. It's one of South America's truly gorgeous places. At the time we were there it was being restored and the main façade was covered in scaffolding, but it didn't matter at all. Neo-classical in style, built from imported European materials, designed in Portugal, it yet looks like nothing Europe has to offer. Joseph Woodroffe, who had such a miserable time in Iquitos, fell in love with Manaus and the 'almost barbaric splendour' of its theatre. It is fashioned in fine white stone, but it's the dome that invites talk of barbarism. In green, blue, and gold, the Brazilian national colours, it can be seen from all over the city and, under the tropical sun, only a few degrees from the equator, it burns with pride and new wealth.

Originally, the theatre was to have had a staircase of Carrara marble; that hope foundered in a shipwreck. But it had Venetian chandeliers, Sèvres porcelain, and ironwork from Glasgow. Under the restorers they were now bringing in yards of French red velvet for new seating and they were digging up the paving stones to lay bare the old latex-covered cobbles that used to dampen the noise of horse-drawn carriages. 'Excuse for the disturbing', said a sign, 'but we are repairing our artistic patrimony. We hope you understand up. Thanks.' A little further away, another sign: 'Amazonas will execut its great destiny. Thanks.'

This was the third major restoration of the century. The building was being eaten away by woodworm and mould, and one of the greatest theatres in the world was living hand-to-mouth on rock concerts and indoor football. Now hope was everywhere. Opera was to return to Manaus for the first time in over eighty years. In 1990 Placido Domingo was to sing at a first night of *Carmen* and a new grand season would begin. But the hope foundered. Brazil's worsening finances put an end to all the plans and, two weeks after the re-opening, the Teatro Amazonas closed its doors.

Much of the romance attached to Manaus and its Opera House came from the surrounding jungle. To the sophisticated onlooker there was always something magical about a theatre in the midst of darkness. It was a victory of civilisation over nature, the proof that European values could survive even in the worst of places. Inside the building, the fine wooden floor of the *salão nobre*, the clusters of columns, the allegorical paintings, the dryads and naiads, all confirmed the undying strength of a tradition already hundreds of years old.

Some of that romance has gone now. Modern Manaus is a place of a million people and the jungle is only the city's playground or an overgrown kitchen garden. No longer hostile, the jungle is marketed everywhere you go, 'protected and preserved for you', as the sign in our hotel says. In the depths of the forest you can go fishing 'in a natural lake', go for rides in a motorised canoe, or spend the day at a mini zoo.

Meanwhile, Manaus is booming. It's a Free Zone to which Brazilians come to buy their video recorders, computers, cameras, and jewelry. Eighty per cent of all electronic consumer goods in Brazil are supplied through Manaus. The roads are dizzy with heat and movement. First World roads of the kind you never see in Peru. There are traffic jams in the rush hour, filling the river air with a soft blue haze. There are cars with blackened windows and air-conditioning: they shield you from the city smells and the thousands camping in the heat under the tin roofs of the shanty towns.

An anthropologist from Berkeley, interviewed in the local paper, said that 'notions of heterosexuality and homosexuality are relatively new in Brazil'. I'm sure he's right, but here in Manaus sexual preferences seem adroitly polarised. Women clatter noisily down the street, their feet tipped like arrow-heads. They sweep the ground before them with a mix of curiosity and indifference, sometimes taking a fragment of extra time to add speculation to observation. While the cowboys of the jungle hunt them out on large motorbikes, muscles tattooed, transistor radio clamped to one ear, and the absolute assurance of being seen.

Two years after we'd been to Manaus Jane wrote to me from a West African city just as stifling, remembering how it was: 'The heat, of course. It seemed unbearable at the time . . . And the unbelievable number of glamorous women. Even when they were doing ordinary things, they looked like models about to go on to the catwalk. I never knew you could be glamorous eating pizza. It was hard to believe they were real. All those short black leather skirts and their fabulous legs and the complicated boots and sandals they wore.'

Manaus takes its name from one of the most famous tribes of the Río Negro. Their homeland was 300 or 400 miles upstream of the modern city. But they once traded all the way down the river and over a vast area of the Amazon basin. The Río Negro is a luxuriant river, almost free of insects. Its dark blue waters are poor in nutrients and unfriendly to mosquitoes. It comes down from the Guayana highlands, a very old and weathered geological zone that gives off little sediment. The waters of the main stream of the Amazon, on the other hand, are muddy and yellow from the mass of deposits brought down from the much younger and less eroded slopes of the Andes.

A few miles downstream of Manaus, the two rivers collide in one of the great tourist attractions of the area. They flow side by side without mixing, yellow on blue, keeping their separate identity for four miles. The Negro moves at almost exactly half the speed of the main stream, looking like a long oil slick beside the Amazon, until finally engulfed, like everything else, by a river big as the sea, but calm and languid.

Aguirre and his men left the Village of the Massacre on 25 May 1561. They passed the confluence of the Negro and the Amazon some time during the following week. They travelled for eight days and seven nights without rest, until they reached another Indian village. Here they found hundreds of dead iguanas, tied by the neck and stored in the huts for food.

Further downstream they came to a Carib village where, for the first time, they saw unmistakable evidence of cannibalism. They found chopping blocks and shreds of butchered flesh. They saw two huts which seemed to them to be places of worship and sacrifice. Each hut had two doors, on one of which was a drawing of a man lying crucified under the sun and, on the other, a woman lying beneath the moon. There were thick bloodstains by each door.

As the Spaniards entered this village, the Indians fled, leaving two of their number behind. The Spanish were curious about their weapons and experimented to see if they were poisonous. They wounded one of the Indians with his own arrows and were intrigued when, within twenty-four hours, he had died in terrible pain, from which 'it was seen that the poison used here was most powerful'.

The chroniclers do not say much about the last thousand

miles from the mouth of the Negro to the sea. They give passing details of places or people, but no overall picture. The expedition must have been in difficulties. Orellana's men, far fewer in number, had nearly starved to death during the final stages of their descent. At one point they had shared out their last ears of corn, one by one. Aguirre seems to have found, as Orellana had done, that the scale of the river's demands overcame all his efforts to impose order on it. But we have no idea what happened to him at this time. He is increasingly alone, withdrawn from the gaze of the chroniclers, and, after the death of don Fernando, he did not leave his ship until they arrived on Margarita Island.

Gradually, on this journey downriver, his confidence in the future must have ebbed away, leaving only a determination to carry on fighting until death. From what we hear about him later on, and from the letter he wrote to Philip II two weeks before his death, we can guess at the depth of his disappointment. He was old and his last chance of achieving something had been mocked by a voyage that must increasingly have seemed as senseless to him as everything that had gone before.

From early June, still 500 miles from the river's mouth, they noticed the tidal effect of the approaching sea. Soon they began to find salt in the villages, for the first time since leaving the land of the Caperuzos nine months before. Aguirre continued with his policy of terror, but the killings now seem to have been less tactical, more driven by a growing paranoia and despair.

Now, when he killed someone, he would say to those watching: '*Ea, caballeros, macheteros delante*' ('Come now, gentlemen, machete-bearers first'). By which he meant, according to Gonzalo de Zúñiga, that he was sending his victims on ahead to clear the path towards death, recognising that soon they would all be going the same way.

He killed a Flemish man named Monteverde, on suspicion that he was guilty of Lutheranism. This was a fashionable heresy of the time. The discovery of Protestant sects in

Valladolid and Seville in the late 1550s had brought such repression to Spain that the Archbishop of Toledo himself was accused of being a heretic. Aguirre then killed Juan Cabañas, a Diego or Pedro de Trujillo, and Juan González. And he ordered Anton Llamoso to put an end to the *comendador* Juan de Guevara: he was stabbed between the shoulder blades and thrown overboard to drown.

They now had to fight their way through Indian settlements; and, for six days, they lost their way among islands, confused and terrified by the changes of current and the movement of the tides. On 30 June, faced with the prospect of a sea journey whose length he could not calculate, Aguirre gave the order to abandon most of the Indian servants they had brought from Peru. They were Christianised Indians who had served the Spanish all the way down the river. Some of the women were pregnant by the Spanish soldiery. Now they were left on the river bank, where their fate could only be death – through disease, hunger, or cannibalism.

Two of the Spaniards were moved to pity at the sight of their desolation. One of them, Diego Palomo, knelt down in front of Aguirre and begged to be allowed to stay behind with the Indians and teach them the Christian faith. But the gesture was hopeless, even though, says Ortiguera, Palomo spoke 'with a humility and simplicity that would have softened a heart of steel'. Both Spaniards were instantly garrotted.

By the beginning of July, it was obvious that they were very close to the sea. Vázquez tells of a party of Spaniards who had gone fishing in a canoe and were swept away by a great storm; and of another party who were drowned by the rising tide. The tide comes, he wrote, 'with such speed and such noise that it can be heard more than four leagues [fourteen miles] away, with a crest of water towering upwards higher than a house'. At last, on 4 July 1561, they reached the Atlantic Ocean and there they gave thanks to God 'for having delivered them from the river'.

Looking back on it all, Francisco Vázquez remembered more than anything the misery of the river's size; how it dominated their lives to the point where even the violence faded into insignificance. They had suffered for nine months, from illness, starvation, and fatigue. Many of the most prominent men had been killed. And yet they had done none of the things they had set out to do. There had been no exploration, no gold and silver, no rich lands to settle and call home.

The river had made them passive and strangely inactive. All they had done in the end was to follow its course, blindly, and without hope. They had changed one not very effective leader for someone who had now shown himself bereft of reason, a psychopath who yet was telling them what they knew to be the truth: that there was no future for them on the river and only death as traitors for most of them in Peru. They were weak from hunger and dispirited, and if Aguirre could prevent them saying so in public, not even he could silence the doubts within.

All the early travellers on the Amazon suffered. To survive you needed strong reserves, both mentally and physically. The greatest survivor of this period was Gaspar de Carvajal, chronicler of the Orellana expedition. He saw the whole experience as a supreme test of faith. He could reflect on his descent of the Amazon over the rest of his long life and he alone managed to give it meaning and coherence. Here he is describing an incident on the river during which he lost one of his eyes in a battle with Indian forces.

> They hit no one but me, for Our Lord permitted them, because of my faults, to plant an arrow in one of my eyes, the arrow passing through my head and sticking out two fingers' length on the other side behind my ear and slightly above it; from which wound I have lost the eye and [even now] I am not without suffering nor free from pain, although our Lord, without my deserving it, has been kind enough to grant me life, so that I may mend my ways and serve Him better . . .

But Carvajal never returned to the Amazon. Unlike Orellana himself, who, having survived the river once, came back to die there in November 1546.

For two days after they left the mouth of the Amazon, Aguirre and his men sailed on through the ocean of fresh water pushed out by the river's enormous flow. On 18 July, the fourteenth day of sailing, they came in sight of Trinidad and on 21 July, at dusk, they saw the island of Margarita. Here Aguirre's wrath fell on a largely defenceless civilian population, and its intensity was such that, over 400 years later, the story of his brief passing has not been forgotten.

# EIGHT

... so great a plague and mortality of men was never remembered to have happened in any place before. For at
first neither were the physicians able to cure it, through
ignorance of what it was, but died fastest themselves, as
being the men that most approached the sick; nor any
other art of man availed whatsoever. All supplications to
the gods, and enquiries of oracles, and whatsoever other
means they used of that kind, proved all unprofitable; in-
asmuch as subdued with the greatness of the evil, they
gave them all over.

*Hobbes's Thucydides*

ANOPHELES. Unprofitable mosquito ... Of all the world's
infectious diseases, malaria is probably the most common.
Peru alone reports over 30,000 cases a year. But until the chills
and fever, the shivering and sweating, the headaches and thirst
arrive on your doorstep, it seems an exotic and faraway sickness. We had gone only a day's sailing from Manaus when Jane
fell ill and the aftermath of some anonymous encounter on the
Upper Amazon sent us back upstream the way we'd come.

The malaria clinic in Manaus is one of the best in South
America. They did what they could, but we did no more serious
travelling after that. We took a plane to Trinidad and spent a
week there in a small hotel on Amethyst Drive, El Dorado. We
ate English food for breakfast, and watched boys playing cricket

in the street, and fell back gratefully into a language that was ours again. Then, at the beginning of October, we flew on to Margarita Island.

Half the world has swarmed over Margarita. The original inhabitants of the island were *guaiqueríes* Indians, a few of whom still survived a hundred years ago. For generations they lived there in peace, trading pearls and sea shells with the Indians of the mainland. Then came the Carib tribes, whose ferocious expansion was in full swing when the Europeans arrived to displace them. The first white man to see Margarita was Christopher Columbus. Sailing down the Caribbean coast on 14 August 1498, he passed to the south of the island and gave it its name. Whether he chose it to honour an Austrian princess, as some say, or a lover, as others claim, or because *margarita* is the Spanish word for 'pearl', we shall never know for certain.

Margarita's fortunes in the early sixteenth century rose and fell by its association with the neighbouring island of Cubagua, an arid rock without wildlife or vegetation, which, because of its vast concentrations of oyster beds, became the site of the first European settlement in Venezuela. For a time Margarita fed and supplied the population of Cubagua, as it served the slave traders from Santo Domingo and buccaneers from all over the Caribbean. When Cubagua's wealth declined in the 1540s, the population of Margarita dwindled and when Lope de Aguirre invaded in 1561 the island was poor and sparsely inhabited. From the mid-1570s Margarita enjoyed a golden age of her own, with the farming of the oyster beds. But then in 1626 the Dutch sacked the island and it was abandoned, as the Spanish withdrew to the mainland for protection.

The island slowly recovered and settled down to a quiet life of stockbreeding, fishing, and agriculture. During the nineteenth century, Margarita's ports of Porlamar, Pampatar, and Juangriego sheltered the revolutionary fleet; and on 3 May 1816 the great Liberator, Simón Bolívar, came through Juangriego to be proclaimed Supreme Ruler of Venezuela in the sleepy inland town of Santa Ana. Then, in the twentieth century, tourists discovered Margarita and the final invasion began.

All through the year people arrive in Margarita, from Caracas or Miami. They stream through the airport and harbour, take over fleets of hire cars, and descend on the 200 miles of coastline. Occasionally the weather changes, but never for long. When you first get off the plane, you tell yourself that this white light of eternal summer is the climate of your dreams. Then, after a day or two, you realise that you're always too hot and that until you leave you'll never be cool again. Each morning it's an effort to remember what happened the day before. After a week, it feels like house arrest in the heart of Paradise.

Margarita Island lies about eighteen miles from the mainland of Venezuela. It's almost forty miles in length, with a maximum width of less than twenty. It's divided into two parts, separated by an isthmus barely fifty yards wide. Most of the inhabitants live on the eastern side. To the west is the Peninsula de Macanao, guarded by two conical hills known, since the nineteenth century, as Las Tetas de María Guevara (the Breasts of María Guevara). Macanao is barren and even hotter than the east, with high bare mountains, like the islands of the Cyclades, and deserted, shadeless beaches. It was a natural place of refuge for those who fled before the terror of Aguirre.

Today the main resort is the town of Porlamar (City of the Sea), in the extreme south-east of the island. It's like all the places in the world where people come to eat and drink and forget about normal living. Hotels rise higher and higher to shield your eyes from the sun. The shops sell Persian carpets, Scotch whisky, pearls, and furs. There's a dirty beach with a heavy smell that seems to pass unnoticed. No one comes here alone. There are only couples, brown and healthy. They sit under wide umbrellas by a sea that's warmer than an average bath, surrounded by restaurants with some of the best food in the Caribbean.

Jane and I rented a house in Juangriego on the north coast. From our balcony we could watch pelicans fishing. They would circle so high that you would lose them in the sun, then dive so

166

fast you would expect to hear the rustle of their wings above the rocking of the waveless sea. At dusk they would perch on the side of fishing boats moored out in the bay and sit and wait, until only their ungainly silhouettes remained against the fading sun. When Jane was stronger, we used to go out into the Macanao Peninsula and lie on a white beach where a couple of scrubby trees survived by the shoreline and the hot sand nipped at our heels like an excited puppy.

Everyone who lives on Margarita has heard of Lope de Aguirre. Elsewhere in South America he's often just a name, except to people who are interested in history. But here he's still part of a remembered past. He's honoured by a statue in the museum in the inland capital of La Asunción, a fine Venezuelan colonial town baked dry by the sun.

The statue stands alone in the open air, in a courtyard dense with tropical vegetation. It's a fine statue. Aguirre looks out from among the tangled strands of yellow and green, authoritative in full armour, a sword in his left hand and a scroll in his right. It's the only place in the world where he is officially commemorated and it's strange that it should be here on Margarita. The statue was commissioned earlier this century by one of Venezuela's dictators, a darkly comic tribute from one tyrant to another. It was supposed to stand overlooking the bay where Aguirre landed, but the local people hated the symbolism and kept pulling it down. So now it rests here, safely anchored in the past.


The pilots who brought Aguirre's two brigantines into Margarita had no idea where the main harbour was. They landed Aguirre's ship at a cove named Paraguachí. Today it's a resort village with palm trees along the front, unfinished hotels, and flocks of vultures. But the beach still carries the invader's name: everyone calls it El Tirano. Aguirre's second brigantine, under the command of his *maestre de campo*, Martín Pérez, arrived some miles away on the north coast, perhaps at Juangriego.

Aguirre understood that now they had reached civilisation his hold over his men would be weakened. They had alternatives here and no longer depended on him alone. So he made some examples, to remind them of his strength. He had two of his men garrotted on the beach and sent word to Martín Pérez for the murder of a third man. Meanwhile, the acting governor of Margarita, don Juan Sarmiento de Villandrando, had news of the arrival of the brigantines and sent out a canoe up the coast from Porlamar to investigate.

Aguirre received the governor's envoys with courtesy. He told them he had recently descended the Amazon and that his men were in great need of food. Whereupon the envoys slaughtered two cows. In return, Aguirre gave one of them a silver cup and a scarlet cloak trimmed with gold and silver. The possibility that these strangers were rich intrigued Villandrando and he left Porlamar for Paraguachí with some of the leading citizens of the island. Aguirre received them well in turn, kneeling down to kiss the governor's feet. Villandrando was young, in his early twenties, and easily flattered. He offered to give Aguirre lodgings in Porlamar; worse still, he agreed to let him bring his men and all their weapons.

Suddenly, the governor was under arrest and Aguirre's ragged army had begun their march on Porlamar. They entered the town at noon with shouts of 'Freedom! Freedom! Long live Lope de Aguirre!' They seized the fortress which guarded the town, broke open the royal treasury, destroyed the accounts, and took everything they could find. Aguirre issued a proclamation, ordering all inhabitants to hand over their arms. He burned the small boats in the harbour and requisitioned supplies for the journey ahead: the chroniclers record 600 sheep, 100 bullocks, chickens, olive oil, maize, and yucca. He threw Villandrando and his chief advisers into prison. And the soldiers celebrated their first day in Porlamar with barrels of looted wine.

But while Aguirre took all the usual precautions of an occupying commander, events quickly showed how far his authority was threatened. Men began to desert. Among the first to leave were the chroniclers Gonzalo de Zúñiga and Francisco Vázquez.

They fled into the mountains and remained in hiding there until Aguirre had left the island. Aguirre went into a rage that seemed to have no end.

He hanged his Captain of Munitions, Juan Enríquez de Orellana, and gave the job to Anton Llamoso. He killed one of his closest comrades, the Basque soldier Juanes de Iturriaga, because of his rowdy behaviour on the main square. He took to futile railing against all those who, he said, had wrecked the New World: the Church, all its bishops and archbishops, but especially the friars; the state bureaucrats, all the magistrates and judges, governors and lawyers. He swore he would kill every one he found. And he attacked all immoral women, 'for they were cause of great evil and scandal in the world, and, on account of one whom the governor Ursúa had brought with him, they had killed him and many others'.

But of all the incidents in the early days of Aguirre's occupation of Margarita, the most significant involved one of the most trusted of his Basque captains, Pedro de Monguía.

Soon after landing in Margarita, Aguirre had word of the presence on the Venezuelan coast of a large ship under the command of a crusading Dominican friar, the Provincial Francisco de Montesinos. He immediately sent out Pedro de Monguía with eighteen men in a large sea-going canoe, with orders to capture the ship and bring it back, so that the expedition could sail on in her to the Panamanian Isthmus. It must have seemed an ideal solution to the problems of transport. But it was a foolish move, since Aguirre's only chance of survival depended on secrecy. It was vital that no one knew he had reached Margarita. From now on, his movements would be broadcast all over the Caribbean. And yet he was so certain of the success of this venture that he gave orders to burn the expedition's two brigantines.

A week went by and still Monguía did not return. Aguirre was by turns desperate and vengeful. If Monguía had been killed or taken prisoner, he vowed to kill the entire population of Margarita, even babes at the breast. He would lay waste the earth, he said, and hang a thousand friars; and he would flay

Montesinos alive and turn his skin into a drum, as an example to all. But when the Provincial's ship finally approached the island, towards midday on 2 August, Aguirre discovered that it came under hostile command. For Monguía and all his men had gone over to the royal authorities.

According to Monguía's own account, he had left Porlamar in his canoe and travelled along the south coast of Margarita as far as Punta de Piedras, today the main ferry port. There he had exchanged the canoe for a larger boat and at sunset on 22 or 23 July he and his men had made the short sea crossing to the Araya Peninsula, which shelters the Gulf of Cariaco. Somewhere along the way, he told his companions of his decision to desert Aguirre and to raise the alarm in the nearby port of Maracapana (the future Cumaná).

When they reached Maracapana, they found neither the Provincial nor his ship. They waited. When Montesinos returned and learned their news, he proposed to send an armed force against Aguirre. Monguía and his men agreed to join and, after a few days, a group of over 100 soldiers left Maracapana to wage war in Margarita. The Provincial had a fighting ship equipped with tar barrels, forty harquebusiers, and a party of Indian archers. It was a powerful force, though still no match for the army under Aguirre's command.

The Provincial's ship landed at Punta de Piedras to take on water and the next day lay at anchor off shore to await events. They seem to have remained there for four or five days, perhaps in the hope of attracting men from the island who wanted to join in the fight against Aguirre. But if this was truly the aim, then the Provincial was to be disappointed, for no one on Margarita came to enlist.

That the inhabitants of the island were unwilling to risk their lives in their own defence can be put down to natural fear. But it was also a reflection of the character of the Provincial himself. For, until the arrival of Aguirre altered the whole scheme of things, Montesinos was the most unpopular man in the eastern Caribbean. By a document of September 1559, Philip II had given Montesinos and his Order guardianship over Margarita's

Indians. He had also given him the right to evangelise the Indian population from Maracapana to the mouth of the Amazon, a long stretch of almost completely unknown coast which the leading families of Margarita also coveted.

As happened elsewhere in the Indies, the Spanish on Margarita had enslaved the local Indians, in contravention of the law. Already in 1544 the governing families had approached the royal authorities, requesting that the ban on enslavement should not be applied in Margarita. Black slaves were too expensive, they argued, and without the Indians 'this island cannot be sustained, for there is no work here but farming'. Montesinos was determined to impose his rule. Had he been a diplomat, more of a prelate and less of a fighting man, there might have been a compromise. But he was irascible, arrogant, and abusive.

He had descended on Margarita with his royal authority and the result had been disastrous. The governor had received him with the dignity due to his rank, but, by the time he left the island, relations had completely broken down. The Provincial had even threatened to bombard Porlamar and destroy its citadel, 'swearing that, if he were not a friar, he would burn the town and treat the inhabitants of the island as if they were [all] Lutherans'.

Now the Provincial was back and his ship was anchored off Punta de Piedras. It's not clear how Aguirre responded. With the chroniclers Vázquez and Zúñiga in hiding somewhere on the island and Monguía with the Provincial, almost all the reports of what was happening in Porlamar are at second hand. There is no doubt that, as soon as Aguirre heard of the arrival of Montesinos, he murdered the governor of Margarita and all the leading citizens. He then seems to have marched to Punta de Piedras with a force of sixty harquebusiers. But his visit was brief, either because, as Vázquez suggests, he found the Provincial's ship already under way, or, as Monguía says, because he realised he was outnumbered. Whatever the reason, he returned almost at once to organise the defences of Porlamar.

On 6 August 1561, the Provincial's ship finally raised anchor and headed for Porlamar, arriving the next day at dawn. The atmosphere in the town, as the chroniclers describe or invent it, was alternately one of anguish and of farce. Aguirre became suspicious of his *maestre de campo*, Martín Pérez, and soon had him shot down and then beheaded. This seems to have caused a great uproar in the citadel. A woman named Marina de Trujillo threw herself from one of the windows of the fortress down into the street, where 'she landed very hard', says a chronicler, 'for she was a fat woman, though from fear she did not feel it'. Her flight then provoked Domingo López and Pedro de Angulo to throw themselves off the battlements and head for the hills.

Three of the chroniclers labour, fascinated, over the actions of the new Captain of Munitions, Anton Llamoso. Vázquez says that he fell under Aguirre's suspicion, and that Aguirre said to him: 'And you, my son, they tell me that you, too, wanted to kill your father.' At which Llamoso apparently lay down prostrate over the headless corpse of Martín Pérez. Ortiguera reports that he was heard to utter the words: 'In the service of my prince I shall drink the brains of the traitor who sought to kill him.' It was an impressive demonstration of fidelity to his leader and caused, says Vázquez, 'great admiration to all'.

The Provincial's ship dropped anchor outside Porlamar. The two sides exchanged fire, but, at that distance, there was little chance of either doing damage to the other. The Provincial's ship drew too much water to come in close and it would have been suicidal for him to have tried to fight his way on shore. Instead, he sent a white flag, proposing a conference. Predictably, Aguirre refused. But then, quite unpredictably, he decided to send the Provincial a letter.

This letter still survives. It is witty and ironic as are few public letters of the time. Ironic, above all, at the expense of the Provincial and the warlike ambitions of men of God. Aguirre begins:

Most Magnificent and Very Reverend Sir,

We would rather have welcomed Your Paternity with bouquets of flowers than with harquebuses and artillery fire. For we have been told by many here that you are more than generous in all things. And certainly, by the works you have performed today, we see that you are even more generous than people said, for Your Paternity [has shown himself] such a lover of arms and military exercise. And so we see our superiors with sword in hand reaching to the very summit of virtue and nobility . . .

With a change in tone he goes on to tell of their sufferings since leaving Peru. He offers a threat ('let those who come against us reflect that they come to do battle with the ghosts of dead men') and an implied justification on behalf of them all:

Your soldiers call us traitors . . . [but] to make you understand all that Peru owes us, and the great reason we have for doing what we do, would, I think, be impossible . . .

He offers to send the Provincial copies of all the documents they have signed in the course of their journey down the Amazon; and he denounces the men who have gone over to the Provincial's side. From the dialect of the Andes he finds a marvellous word to describe Monguía and his associates, a word full of contempt as well as nostalgia for the time when they were comrades: the deserters, he says, are all *chafalonía*, meaning worn-out golden jewelry, once valuable but now fit only to be melted down.

Then he savages one of the absent chroniclers: 'And if, by chance', he says, 'a certain Gonzalo de Zúñiga has shown up in your camp, a man from Seville, with bushy eyebrows that meet in the middle, then Your Paternity may know him for a very vulgar man.' He is robber, murderer, and traitor, 'a man who is very industrious when there is something to eat, but always quick to fly whenever there is a fight – though his signatures cannot fly,' he adds slyly, reminding the Provincial that Zúñiga's signature, like that of all the deserters, is on the document drawn up after the death of Pedro de Ursúa.

Aguirre ends his letter with what sounds, in retrospect, like uncanny foreknowledge. He warns Montesinos not to go to Santo Domingo, 'for we know for certain that [there] they will dispossess you of the throne on which you sit'. Then, in a gesture that might have found the common ground between them, Aguirre adds the motto of the Borgias: *Aut Caesar, aut nihil* ('Caesar or nothing'). 'God will punish the traitors, and the King will resurrect the faithful,' he says, in a last ironic flourish, 'though to date we have not seen the King resurrect anyone, nor does he give life or heal wounds . . . From this, our fortress in Margarita, your servant Lope de Aguirre kisses the hands of Your Paternity.'

If the Provincial ever replied to this letter, as Vázquez says he did, all record has been lost. But he seems to have quickly realised that his mission in Margarita was hopeless and he set sail again for Maracapana.

On 15 October 1561, after Aguirre had left the island, a Committee of Inquiry was held in Margarita to examine the role Montesinos had played. Doña Marcela Manrique, widow of the murdered governor, held him responsible for the death of her husband. She argued that, having learned of Aguirre's presence on Margarita, Montesinos should immediately have informed the judicial authorities in Santo Domingo. His attempts at armed intervention, she claimed, had been totally counterproductive. His superiors agreed. The Provincial was removed from office, as Aguirre had predicted, and banished from the Indies in perpetuity.

Yet of all the men who confronted Aguirre, perhaps this warlike friar was the one best suited to the task. He was devious and he did not lack courage. Ten years later, in October 1571, we find the same doña Marcela, now re-married, petitioning the authorities to have Montesinos arrested: he had returned secretly to the Indies and was back on Margarita, though to what end we do not know.

The episode of the Provincial and his ship was a disaster for Aguirre. His plans had always depended on speed. He knew that if he waited more than a few days in Margarita his presence would become known, more men would desert, and he would lose his chance of descending on the Isthmus with a coherent fighting force. Now, with the departure of Montesinos, the authorities in Santo Domingo and all along the coast of Tierra Firme would know what was happening. Worse, Aguirre had destroyed the expedition's only two ships, which condemned them to remain on Margarita for another three weeks while they worked to finish another.

In Porlamar and the surrounding country the reign of terror went on. They killed and burnt and stole. Aguirre murdered Martín Díaz de Almendáriz, a first cousin of Pedro de Ursúa whom he seems to have been keeping alive as a kind of hostage. He stabbed Juan de Aguirre and threw him off the battlements of the fortress. He hanged Ana de Rojas, a woman from Margarita, in the main square. Two Dominican friars suffered the inevitable consequences of his confrontation with Montesinos. One of them, the chroniclers record, was garrotted in a bestial manner, with a rope passed across his mouth rather than around his neck.

At last, on the final day of August, Aguirre's army withdrew from Margarita. They left the island traumatised and impoverished, with all sense of community destroyed.

In his chronicle Vázquez tries to take stock of the expedition he was never to see again. So far, he estimated, Aguirre had killed thirty-nine of the people who had come from Peru; twenty-five of them had died on the Amazon and another fourteen on Margarita. He had arrived on the island with around 200 fighting men. Fifty-seven of these, a quarter of his force, were now gone: dead, deserted, or abandoned as invalids in Porlamar. He apparently picked up a dozen new soldiers on Margarita. So he left for the Venezuelan mainland with about 160 men, as well as a large quantity of swords and lances, six small cannon, 130 harquebuses, saddles for the horses they hoped to find in Venezuela, three horses of their own, and a mule.

Aguirre recognised that the Panamanian Isthmus would now be closed to him and he began to formulate a new plan. They would march through Venezuela and explore the overland route across the Andes back to Peru. It was a measure of almost total lunacy, but it is hard to see what else he could have done, except surrender. The journey was feasible, though not for men in their condition who had already been through so much. In 1546 a group of twenty-five adventurers had left Margarita to travel the route Aguirre now proposed to follow. They had taken two years to reach Tunja in the eastern Cordillera of the Andes, still very far from Peru. They arrived in rags and looked, said an observer, 'little different from savages'.

Aguirre set sail from Porlamar for the port of Nuestra Señora de la Concepción de Borburata, the outlet for the inland town of Valencia, near the modern Puerto Cabello. They had one large ship, completed over the previous three weeks, and three tiny boats. The journey to Borburata should have taken no more than two or three days, but the expedition did not arrive on the mainland until 12 September. Twelve days at sea is an inexplicably long time. The chroniclers talk of calm waters or contrary winds, of Aguirre's indecision as he pondered the welcome which might await him in Borburata, of the pilots' deliberate errors of navigation. But it is still difficult to imagine what can have taken them so long.

The atmosphere on board ship grew calamitous. Aguirre threatened the pilots with death, though he was not a man of the sea and could not manage without them. 'If God had made heaven for such contemptible . . . men as these', he would say, 'then he, Lope de Aguirre, had no wish to go there.' And, at other times, raising his eyes towards the sky, he would say: 'God, if you are going to do me any favour, do it now, and keep the glory for your Saints.'

Aguirre's attitude towards God and religion is an interesting one. It was never consistent, but he seems generally to have thought of God in the way that he thought of the king of Spain: as a powerful lord to whom it was right to pay allegiance, but only so long as the lord protected those beneath him. When the lord failed, then the subject was free to find a better leader, or even to go it alone.

In the fourteenth and fifteenth centuries, the Basque provinces had been torn by the rivalries of feudal lords organised into competing *bandos* or factions, and it is the word *bando* that comes back to Aguirre when he thinks of God. He would say, according to Vázquez, that the only God he could believe in was one who, like himself, was a *bandolero*, a brigand or a bandit. 'Up to a certain moment', he would add, 'he had been a member of [God's] party [*bando*], but . . . now he had passed over to join His enemies.' God had deserted him in time of need, and Aguirre registers this not as a crisis of faith, but as disappointment in the failure of a leader who had once promised his followers so much.

As the expedition drew near to Borburata, they saw a merchant ship lying in the harbour. Ominously, as they watched, its captain gave orders for the ship to be scuttled, which could only mean that their arrival had been anticipated. In his fury Aguirre set fire to the wreck that remained, as he symbolically burnt his own ship, committing them all now to a journey overland.

Aguirre marshalled his forces on the beach and there they spent the night. The next day he sent out scouts inland to explore the nearest settlement. It was deserted, as almost all the settlements on the Amazon had been, and for the same reason. Aguirre murdered a Portuguese soldier named Farías, because he asked whether they had reached the mainland, or whether Borburata was simply another island.

They occupied the deserted settlement and remained for two weeks, until the end of September. Aguirre, conscious that time was passing beyond his control, lived as a recluse, cut off by his personal bodyguard. He gave orders, but rarely appeared. His men went out looking for horses and eventually, after much searching in the heat, brought back between twenty-five and thirty, mostly unbroken mares. Several of the soldiers returned badly wounded from pointed stakes which the retreating inhabitants had set in ambush along the main paths.

Aguirre, desperate for transport, wrote a letter to the people of Valencia, twenty-five miles away. If each of them would contribute a horse, he promised to pass by in peace. If not, he would march on them and burn their town to the ground. He hanged one of his men called Pérez, whom he found lying sick by the side of a stream. They placed a sign around his neck saying *'Por inútil y desaprovechado'* ('for being useless and unproductive'). They found large quantities of wine in the village. They drank it and cooked their meals in it. Some bathed naked in the opened barrels or poured it into troughs to wash their feet at night, which, says Vázquez, 'was certainly a thing of great destruction and a sorry sight to behold'.

With Aguirre's army stalled in Borburata, the royalist forces began to assemble against him. At first they organised the resistance from the town of San Juan Evangelista del Tocuyo, which was the *de facto* capital of Venezuela in the early colonial period. Formal responsibility for the defence of the country rested with the governor there, Pablo Collado. He found himself in a difficult position. He had few fighting men and they were poorly armed. It isn't clear exactly how he responded to the crisis – the details would be the subject of a controversial inquiry held a few weeks after Aguirre's death. But whether from illness, as his doctors reported, or from cowardice, as others said, his personal contribution was to be minimal.

Unable or unwilling to take charge directly, Collado turned to the best commander he had, Gutierre de la Peña. De la Peña would prove himself a shrewd tactician over the weeks to come. He made do with his limited forces, recognising that acts of heroism against a man as desperate as Aguirre would be a needless extravagance.

De la Peña appealed for men to come and fight. In El Tocuyo he had only forty horsemen, armed with lances and ox-hide shields. As the days went by, reinforcements began to arrive, some from as far away as Mérida, 140 miles to the south-west. But even with these extra men, de la Peña would always hold back from meeting Aguirre head on, because of an almost total lack of fire-power. The chroniclers imply that there were no more than a handful of harquebuses in all of Venezuela at the time, and this put the royalists at a crushing disadvantage.

De la Peña knew from deserting soldiers which way Aguirre was likely to come and he prepared to surround him near the town of Nueva Segovia de Barquisimeto, to the north-east of El Tocuyo. He chose a position on the heights overlooking the town and his forces settled down to wait.

A few days later, he was joined by another skilled commander, Diego García de Paredes. The illegitimate son of a man who had been known all over the Spanish world as the 'Samson of Estremadura', García de Paredes had inherited many of the qualities of his famous father. He had come to the New World in the late 1540s and helped to organise the resistance of the Caribbean ports against assaults by French pirates. In 1558 he founded the town of Cuicas which, after a number of changes of location, and a change of name to Trujillo, would become one of the most important cities in Venezuela. Now he was appointed de la Peña's *maestre de campo*. But he would not live long to enjoy the honours of victory: in 1563 he was attacked and eaten by alligators as he rested by the bank of a river.

Aguirre and his men left the settlement of Borburata on 29 September. They had only enough horses to carry their supplies and artillery, so almost everyone had to walk. The path leading south towards Valencia was rough and they had a climb of 1,500 feet into the mountains. Temperatures here can rise as high as anywhere in South America. Aguirre showed enormous determination and physical courage. As men half his age collapsed under their burdens, he took more and more on his own shoulders, aware, above all, that though they might go without food they could never survive without guns and ammunition.

They were four days on the journey. As they neared Valencia, Aguirre's health finally failed him and he was carried into the town on the shoulders of his men, while others shaded his face from the tropical sun. Now, if ever, would have been the time for his soldiers to desert, or kill him, and the chroniclers are at a loss to understand why they did neither. It cannot have been simply fear. There must have been something about this toothless wreck of a man that induced them to keep him alive. Perhaps it was the devil's charisma, the power of a leader who was apparently afraid of nothing; or perhaps they felt that in spite of all he had made them suffer they would be lost once he was no longer with them.

Aguirre should have died in Valencia. But, miraculously, he rose again and dictated a letter to King Philip of Spain by which he will always be remembered.

In principle, there was no reason why a man should not write to his king. It was a custom that had survived from the Middle Ages. Any subject was free to approach the monarch. He could seek justice in cases of dispute, protest about things that troubled him, or simply pass on information he thought was important. Aguirre's letter to Philip II bears the marks of these customary origins. But in content it oversteps all boundaries of what was, or could ever be, possible in relations between a subject and his king.

The letter is not the work of a rational mind. It rambles, shifts constantly in tone, from arrogance to self-abasement, and it lacks the wit of the letter to Montesinos. But it is still one of the strangest and most fascinating documents of its time. It begins,

> King Philip, native of Spain, son of Charles, Invincible,
>
> Lope de Aguirre, your humblest vassal, an old Christian, of undistinguished parents, *hidalgo*, native of the Basque country in the kingdom of Spain, citizen of the town of Oñate: in my youth I crossed the Ocean Sea to the lands of Peru, to show my greater worth with lance in hand . . . ; and so, for twenty-four years, I have done you great service in Peru, in the conquests of Indians and the colonising of cities . . .

All this is simply formal. But the letter then goes off in many directions. At times Aguirre remains the loyal subject, reminding his king of past services to the crown; of how he fought at the battle of Chuquinca under Alonso de Alvarado and how he was wounded in the leg by two shots from a harquebus. At other times Aguirre howls at the insolence of the king's officers or the depradations of the friars. Sometimes he seems to feel that the king is good and wise, let down only by the ambition and corruption of his advisers. But his hostility can suddenly become personal: 'I hold it for certain that few kings ever go to hell. But that is [only] because you are so few in number; for if you were many, none of you could ever get to heaven. For I believe that there you would be worse than Lucifer, since you hunger and thirst . . . to satiate yourselves on human blood.'

He relives, for the king, the moment of his declaration on the Amazon:

> Be advised, Spanish king . . . [that] I, along with those companions whose names I shall shortly give you, have effectively abandoned all allegiance to you, and, denaturalising ourselves from our homeland, which is Spain, we here make on you the most merciless war that our strength can suffer and sustain. And this, believe it, king and lord, we have been brought to do because we cannot bear the great taxes . . . and the unjust punishments which these your ministers impose on us . . .

This is the pain of a man who cannot accept that a quarter of a century of hardship can have led to so little. But in his anger and self-pity Aguirre also begins to discover a language which will one day return in the mouths of saner rebels.

> Hear me! Hear me! Spanish king. Do not be cruel to your vassals, nor ungrateful. For while you and your father were in the kingdom of Castile, free from cares, your vassals won for you, at the cost of their blood and their livelihood, all the kingdoms and estates that you have in these parts. And hear me! king and lord. You cannot rightfully draw any revenue from these lands, where you yourself have risked nothing, until those who have laboured here have been rewarded.

Through all the confusions of a mind that has recently come very near to death, the central political charge survives: that the mother land grows unfairly rich, while those who have laboured to build the colonies are left to die in poverty.

Aguirre then goes on to give his own summary of the

Amazon adventure, a laconic detailing of incidents that now hold no interest for him and might almost have happened to someone else:

> In the year 1559, the marquis of Cañete entrusted the expedition of the river of the Amazons to Pedro de Ursúa, a Navarrese, or, to tell the truth, a Frenchman; and he delayed the building of his ships until 1560, in the Province of the Motilones, which is a district of Peru. Because the Indians go about with their heads shaved, they are called Motilones. But most of these ships fell apart as soon as they were launched, for the country where they were built is very wet, and we made rafts and we left the horses and the cattle behind, and we descended the river . . .
>
> This governor [Ursúa] was so wicked, ambitious, and mean that we could not bear it; and so . . . we killed him . . . and then we raised a young gentleman of Seville, named don Fernando de Guzmán, to be our king . . . and they named me as his *maestre de campo*; and because I did not consent to their insults and their evil deeds, they wanted to kill me, and so I killed the new king and the Captain of his Guard, and his Lieutenant-General, and four Captains, and his Steward, and his Chaplain, who said mass, and a woman, who was in league against me, and a Knight Commander of Rhodes, and an Admiral and two ensigns, and five or six others of their allies. It was my intention to carry on the war and to die in it, on account of the many cruelties which your ministers have committed against us. And I named new Captains and a Sergeant-Major, and they wanted to kill me, and so I hanged them all. And we continued our course, while all these deaths and ill-luck befell us on the Río Marañón, and it was more than ten-and-a-half months before we reached the mouth of the river and the sea . . . God knows how we escaped from that fearful lake . . .

Aguirre spares himself nothing in this catalogue of events. Each incident, each death, has its own logic, but the whole adds up to a meaningless flow of wasted time. He ends his letter with a list of the soldiers currently under his command and he signs himself: 'Son of faithful vassals from the Basque country, and rebel unto death because of your ingratitude, Lope de Aguirre, *The Wanderer.*'

There may have been monarchs in history who would have been amused by Aguirre's letter, as a curiosity to pass a dull moment between pressing affairs of state. But Philip II was certainly not one of them. In 1561 he was no longer the handsome youth painted by Titian, but he was still far from the old man who would die worn out by dysentery, gout, and malaria. He was dour, hard-working, consumed by the task of consolidating the kingdom of Spain as the greatest power in the world. He had no time for curiosities. But, in any case, his bureaucracy was no doubt efficient enough to ensure that Aguirre's letter never reached him.

Aguirre and his men spent twelve days in Valencia, while the royalist forces waited for him outside Barquisimeto. Valencia was a pleasant place to stay. Founded in 1553, it was quickly growing to become one of the most important towns in Venezuela, on account of the trade which it controlled through the port of Borburata. An early eighteenth-century observer wrote:

> Valencia is situated on a height overlooking a most beautiful plain, in sight of a lake more than sixteen leagues in length and five or six wide. Endowed with many fish, birds, and every kind of game, it is a lovely site, luxuriant and agreeable . . .

Today, Valencia is the third largest city in Venezuela. It is heavily industrialised and its great lake is inevitably polluted. But it still benefits from the trade in agricultural products and its oranges are as famous as those from Valencia in Spain.

On 15 October, Aguirre's forces left for Barquisimeto by a path through the *sierra*, leaving Valencia in flames behind them. Once again their journey was long and difficult. The path was rocky and passed through thick forest. Ten soldiers deserted along the way. Heavy rain fell and the pack animals foundered on the muddy slopes. Vázquez writes:

> At this, [Aguirre] uttered so many blasphemies against God and His Saints that all who heard him were filled with terror; and he said in his fury: 'Does God think that because it rains in torrents I shall not return to Peru and destroy the world? If so, He is mistaken in me . . .'

They entered the deserted town of Barquisimeto on 23 October and set it alight. As with most places in colonial Venezuela, the buildings were entirely of wood with straw-thatched roofs, and they burned easily. One of the 'portable towns' that were common in the early history of Venezuela, Barquisimeto had already moved once since its founding in 1552. After it was destroyed in 1561 it would move twice more, until it came to occupy its present position, 1,800 feet up in the *sierra*, on the heights where once the royalist forces lay in wait for Aguirre's approaching army.

With Aguirre in possession of the ruined town, the governor Pablo Collado wrote to him, offering a free pardon to all who would give up the fight and go over to the royalist side. This was to be a dangerous move for Collado personally, one that would nearly cost him his life when the scores came to be settled after Aguirre's death. But, at the time, it was fully supported by the judicial authorities in Santo Domingo. Their official view was that most of the soldiers in Aguirre's army had been driven to take part against their will; while, unofficially, they no doubt recognised that diplomacy was a better way to handle a situation in which the opposing army held all the best weapons.

Aguirre sent a confused reply to Collado's letter. He turned aside all talk of pardons, saying that 'we are a people with little desire to live'. He apologised for burning down the church in Barquisimeto and asked for the return of three mules and a colt that had somewhere been taken from him. Yet still he played to his men. He rode about the camp on a black horse. His banner was of black silk crossed by two bloody swords. He cajoled and encouraged, tried to find reasons for carrying on, while his army began to melt away around him. The mood in the camp soon turned to complete despair. They were hemmed in by the royalists and increasingly hungry. They ate their dogs and horses, as once they had done on the Amazon, and every day more men deserted.

The attrition could have only one end, and it came on Monday 27 October 1561. Cut off in Barquisimeto, Aguirre proposed to fight his way back to Borburata and try his luck again on the sea. It was a hopeless gesture and the soldiers refused to follow him. 'If it is my fate to die ruined in this land of Venezuela', he said, 'then I believe neither in the word of God, nor in the sect of Mahomet, nor in Luther, nor in the pagan world: I believe that there is nothing for man except birth and death.' As his army escaped to join the royalists, Aguirre was left with half a dozen men, including the faithful Portuguese shoemaker Anton Llamoso. 'How does it seem to you, my son?' Aguirre asked him. And Llamoso replied: 'I think I am going to die with you. But I will stay until we are cut to pieces.'

Aguirre watched as García de Paredes finally began to close in on him. And at this point he turned to his daughter, Elvira, who had been with him all the way from Peru. She has hardly been mentioned by the chroniclers until now and we know nothing about her. One observer tells us she was 'a young girl, of gentle disposition, and beautiful'. Her mother was an anonymous Indian woman, perhaps from Peru or some other country, like Nicaragua, where Aguirre failed to leave his mark. Elvira – the name means 'joyful and faithful' – was of marriageable age, perhaps thirteen or fourteen.

Aguirre withdrew into a ruined hut where she was sheltering from the confusion, and he prepared her for what was to come.

> My daughter, my love. I thought I should see you married and a great lady. But my sins and my great pride have willed it otherwise ... Commend yourself to God, my daughter, and make your peace with Him. For it is not right that you should remain in this world for some villain

to enjoy your beauty and your loveliness, or to insult you, calling you daughter of the traitor Lope de Aguirre.

Elvira went down on her knees and begged for life: 'I shall become a nun where neither sky, nor sun, nor moon shall ever see me . . . There I shall pray to God for you and for me . . .' Then Aguirre stabbed her until she died. The chroniclers suggest that she was the only person Aguirre ever loved in the world, and there is no reason to doubt it. At the hour of his death he could not bear the thought of her surviving to become, as he said in a memorable phrase, 'a mere mattress for the unworthy'.

After Elvira was dead, Aguirre made no attempt to defend himself. He threw down his weapons and waited. The chroniclers are not sure how he died. He apparently offered to give himself up, but it seems as if two of his former soldiers took the law into their own hands and shot him down before the governor could arrive to accept his surrender. They say he was shot twice with a harquebus. That after the first shot he sighed and said: 'That was nothing'; and after the second: 'That will do,' and fell to the floor.

The chronicler Custodio Hernández was there to cut off his head. He took it by the hair, 'which was very long', and brought it out to show the governor. Later it was taken to El Tocuyo and placed in an iron cage, 'where it remained many days as a warning to evil-doers', says another of the chroniclers. 'His skull is still at the same place, with his banners, and also the bodice and mantle of yellow silk worn by his daughter when [he] killed her. You can still see the dagger marks in them.'

The body of Aguirre was quartered and thrown into the street. His hands were cut off and carried off on the point of a lance, as if, says Vázquez, 'they were the relics of a saint'. But, he adds, 'it seems to me that it would have been better to have thrown him to the dogs, that they might have eaten him whole, and thus the memory of his evil fame might [more quickly] have perished'. The left hand was given to the people of

Valencia and the right to the town of Mérida. It was said that the soldiers going to Valencia threw the left hand to their dogs, while those going down to Mérida, a long journey to the southwest, were overcome by the terrible smell of rotting flesh and threw the right hand into a river.

With the benefit of their free pardons, Aguirre's men soon dispersed throughout Venezuela. But as the horrors of the past months became clearer, some of the state officials decided on vengeance. Collado was the inevitable scapegoat. Even before news of Aguirre's death reached Santo Domingo, a decision had been taken to replace him as governor. Now he was brought before a judicial tribunal and, in December 1561, he was sentenced to death for cowardice. This would later be commuted to a term of imprisonment, but he was released a broken man, his reputation destroyed, his health and finances in ruins.

One by one Aguirre's former soldiers were rounded up, though we know little of the details. Anton Llamoso was discovered in the Andes, in Pedro de Ursúa's town of Pamplona. He was quartered and his head displayed in the main square. The chronicler Gonzalo de Zúñiga was captured and taken to prison in Santo Domingo. Later he was sent to Spain, where he was sentenced to perpetual banishment from the Indies. Of Pedro de Monguía and Francisco Vázquez, we hear no more. But Custodio Hernández was one of a group of fifteen former *marañones* who were picked up in Valencia in January 1562 to be sent on to Santo Domingo and an unknown fate.

About Aguirre himself the chroniclers have no doubts. His soul, says Vázquez, 'went down into hell for ever', as the 'most evil and wicked man that was ever born on earth'. He was 'a man of almost fifty years of age, very small . . . [and] gaunt. When he looked at you fixedly', Vázquez remembered, 'his eyes would be agitated, especially when he was angry, and his mind was sharp and quick for someone who was unlettered.'

Aguirre would not have been surprised at his fate. He used to say that his soul was beyond saving and that he would burn in hell. Yet this passive despair, which is so closely linked to his love of the theatrical, was always in conflict with his belief that he was made for the world and that the world was made for action. In his rebellious moods, Aguirre, like Satan, refused to serve. He could not accept that he had come too late to win the inheritance of the Indies. He would take Adam's will and show it to the king of Castile, he once said, to see whether Adam had ever bequeathed the New World to the crown of Spain.

When his energy deserted him, however, there was only darkness and a lingering concern for reputation. Aguirre was not the first or the last to understand that the cloak of the villain was the surest guarantee of immortality. 'For he had often said that, if he could not return to Peru and lay it waste, and kill all those who lived there, then at least the fame of all the things he had done and all his cruelties would remain in the memory of man for ever.'

He was right, of course, for he was never forgotten. For many years the city of El Tocuyo held an annual celebration on the day of Aguirre's death. And, by the end of the eighteenth century, he was firmly established as one of the wild men of South American mythology. The explorer Alexander von Humboldt recorded the following note:

> At Cumaná [the former Maracapana], before the earth-quake of 14 December 1797, a strong smell of sulphur was perceived near the hill of the convent of Saint Francis. At the same time, flames appeared on the banks of the Manzanares and in the gulf of Cariaco . . . This last pheno-menon is quite frequent in the Alpine calcareous mountains near Cumanacou and in the island of Margarita, where flakes of fire rise to a considerable height.
>
> This fire, which is like the will-o'-the-wisp of our marshes, does not burn the grass. The people call these reddish flames 'the soul of the traitor Aguirre', and the natives of Barquisimeto believe that the soul of the traitor wanders in the savannahs, like a flame that flies the approach of men.

# EPILOGUE

He was borne in Biskay, a countrey neere unto France,
wherefore I beleeve him rather to have beene a Frenchman
than a Spaniard, for that in the heart of a Spaniard could
not be so much crueltie as this man shewed.

*A Discourse of the West Indies . . .*
*Written by López Vaz, a Portugall*

Elsewhere in the world nights grew longer and the seasons
changed. But through October and November Jane and I
waited on in the wet heat of Margarita's endless summer. We
swam every day from the same deserted beach and sheltered
from the hottest hours in the shadow of a stunted tree that
whistled in the breeze from off the sea. Then December brought
refugees from the north. City people, who began to arrive in
large numbers, fleeing before the season's festivities. Groups of
men in baseball caps and Bermuda shorts, with plastic bags that
strained under their duty-free liquor; couples from the Mid-
West, from Minneapolis and Sioux Falls, bearing tales of early
snow; shy lovers, suddenly alone and troubled. They looked
very pale on the beaches and they filled the restaurants with
their laughter and aimless energy, the language and smell of a
familiar world.

So we left Margarita Island. Jane went north to spend Christmas in the highlands of Guatemala. I flew to Caracas and took a

bus across Venezuela towards the Andes. We passed orange
groves on the way to Valencia and there were great herds of beef
cattle, head down in good grazing country. At Barquisimeto I
stopped and spent the night – but only for the association, for
the city was destroyed by an earthquake in 1812 and is without a
past. Then I travelled down to Mérida, through the vineyards
by El Tocuyo on the edge of the *cordillera*. The highest
mountains were snow-covered. It was good to breathe cool air
again and I was glad to be going home. On 23 December I
crossed the frontier into Colombia, where a lonely official, glad
to intrude, picked over the debris of the past few months: some
photographs and sketches, a few colourful banknotes – the
lightest and cheapest of souvenirs – a stack of accumulated visit-
ing cards, and a plane ticket from Bogotá to London.

Four years later, in the summer of 1991, Jane and I met again, in
the south of Spain. She was coming home to England from
North Africa and we shared the drive from Algeciras. It was
mid-July and the peninsula was walled in by the heat. We drove
at night and slept during the day. Then, as we came towards
Burgos in the early morning, it was suddenly cooler. We
crossed the Ebro in mist and rain and stopped in Vitoria, which
is the capital of the Basque province of Alava.

We were tired and looked for somewhere to sleep. But Vitoria was celebrating. It was full in the way only Spanish towns
can be full, a chaos of hats and voices, marching bands and bark-
ing dogs, with the air tasting of motorbikes and *churros*. There is
nowhere else to stay on the way north until you reach Guernica
or Bilbao. But closer than either of these is the town of Oñate,
thirty miles to the north-east.

Since I had returned from South America I had thought less
and less about Aguirre. Other people and places had intervened.
He had become a distant and exotic figure, too eccentric, too
large to fit into the cramped spaces of Europe. But in their home
town everyone is cut down to size; and so I found myself in
Oñate facing, not the monster of the Amazon, but the much
more manageable portrait of the eternal boy next door.

The best way to approach Oñate is from the south-east. That way you come along a winding road through old forests of beech and oak, past tumbling streams and stray farmhouses, or tiny hamlets with Basque names: Zegama, Zerain, Aztiria. But if you come from Vitoria the approach is desolate. You leave by the Calle Portal de Gamarra, an ugly street lined with Basque graffiti and the stumps of butchered trees. After seven miles the road forks towards Bergara. You cross the Alava plain, bleak in the sun, bleaker in the rain, the home of junk lots, old tyres, and scraps of rusting metal.

After ten miles you pass into the Basque province of Guipúzcoa and soon afterwards you reach the industrial belt at a place called Arrasate in Spanish and Mondragon in Basque. Then your first sight of Oñate is through a web of electric power-lines, an outer ring of corrugated iron, car salesrooms, and decayed factories.

Oñate lies in a valley. If you come in winter there is often snow on the mountains, which rise to over 4,000 feet. The rest of the year, even in high summer, the land is damp and green. This is the classic scenery of the northern Basque country, of narrow valleys locked between high mountains. No soil for the plough, unlike the open country of the Basque south, rich in wine and olives.

Seeing Oñate, I thought of Aguirre in one of his sentimental moods: 'If only they'd given us some wretched job or other,' he wrote to the Provincial Montesinos, 'we could have put order into our lives.' We only wanted a bit of land, he went on, 'however miserable it was, [somewhere] we could stop and rest these sad bodies of ours that are more patched than a pilgrim's cloak.'

For almost half a millennium Europe exported her poverty and her dreams, sending people across the world in the hope of better times. Aguirre's is the voice of the many who never made it. But in his anguish he was also a prophet. The Spain of his time was growing rich on the plunder of the Indies; but, by turning her back on the sweat of those who had made the Indies possible, she was opening the way to her long decline. Increasingly, her successful men would send their sons to cultivate respectability in the law or the church, leaving only a place of scorn for those who believed in working with their hands.

All that is most beautiful in Oñate today – the stonework of the university or the great convent of Bidaurreta – is symbolic of the Spain Aguirre hated. The greatest power on earth in the sixteenth century, she would enter the twentieth as a byword for ignorance and poverty, a picturesque land of priests, donkeys, and beggars that I knew as a child.

Now most of the donkeys and beggars have gone and Spain grows rich again. Today Aguirre would have less cause to leave. I think of him as just another commuter, to the sprawling complex at Mondragon or a busy office in Alava. I can't believe he would have joined ETA and become a terrorist – he wasn't the sort to join things. But as a sixteenth-century wanderer and rebel against Madrid he has a place among the favourite sons of Oñate.

The local guidebook says nothing of his crimes or the violence on the Amazon. He is one of the few *oñatiarras* to have made a name in the world and that is enough. In the dependent hamlet of Araotz, five miles from the city centre, you can see a house that may once have been his; and an old man we met coming up the valley in the mist of early evening remembered a banquet there thirty years before, in memory of the four hundredth anniversary of his death.

Leaving Aguirre among friends, we crossed into Navarre in search of his old enemy. Seven miles from the French frontier, off the N121, is the village of Arizkun and the house of Pedro de Ursúa in the Baztán valley. We arrived at the end of a day of unceasing rain. The Pyrenees were hidden in swirls of cloud that by the next morning had reached down almost to the valley floor. Swifts were feeding on the damp air, children were playing around the *frontón* court, and there was the warm smell of wet animals and straw that is one of the most welcoming in the world.

There are a few new buildings on the outskirts of Arizkun, pretty Swiss chalets drowned in flowers. But the centre still has the old houses, massive blocks of peeling pink stone that sit right to the edge of the street, with shuttered windows and cows grazing at the back door. They have red-tiled roofs and each has its coat of arms over the entrance. Opposite the *frontón* court is the only place to stay, a dark and friendly *posada*, with old oak and old-fashioned mountain cooking.

The house of Pedro de Ursúa looks down on Arizkun from the north, in the Barrio Bozate. It was already 200 years old when he was born. Once a fortified stronghold, it was domesticated by additions in the seventeenth century and now looks altogether like the solid Basque farmhouse it has become. Late in July it was still shearing time. The courtyard of the house was filled with the bleating of sheep. And on the terrace above, where once men must have passed the hours on watch, there was no one, only a small fig tree in a broken pot, a row of geraniums, and two marijuana plants leaning from an old shopping basket.

The Ursúa family had its share of misery, though perhaps no greater than they would have thought usual for the age. Pedro's father was named Tristan, after the fashion of the chivalric romances that still fascinated the Spanish nobility on the eve of the Conquest. Tristan's eldest son, Miguel, died in a duel, his second son, Pedro, by the shores of the Amazon, his youngest, Juan, from wounds received in jousting at Valladolid.

An aristocracy worthy of the name. But the way of life has little to say to us, surviving only as an afterglow of romance. Aguirre, as the victor, speaks more directly, through the still unreconciled daring of his madness and the bleak vision of his solitary meritocracy. 'For now that we no longer believe in God', he wrote to the prelate Montesinos, 'the man who is worth no more than the next is worth nothing at all.'

The Baztán valley is a quiet place. A few tourists stop over on their way south to Pamplona, but the climate is too independent to keep them long. On our last morning in Arizkun we climbed up to the Col d'Ispéguy and watched griffon vultures drifting with the clouds across the border. Fifty years ago people risked their lives here. Now there's only a marker by the road and an empty customs post, a relic of old Europe to show the children on a day's outing from Saint-Jean-Pied-de-Port.

It was a day of fierce sunshine. We had Spanish wine and French bread. In the afternoon we slept for a while in a grove of fir trees, and then we drove on over the mountains into France.

# A NOTE ON THE
CHRONICLERS

THE CHRONICLERS of the Aguirre expedition left surprisingly coherent accounts of it. Naturally, they don't always agree with each other. They moralise, they exaggerate, they invent. But they do seem to be telling the same story.

Not that this coherence is wholly reassuring. For one thing, it is clear that in the aftermath of Aguirre's treachery there was an official line to be toed by any prudent writer, and particuarly so in the case of those chroniclers who, like Francisco Vázquez, were writing to save their own skins. For another, it is certain that some of the chroniclers had access to the writings of the others. Nevertheless, they have left us with enough to put a story together.

One of the best accounts is by Toribio de Ortiguera. He was not an eye-witness to any of the events he describes and he sometimes wants to tell what should have happened, rather than what did. But he worked hard and had good sources. Ortiguera was in Panama in the service of the king of Spain in the 1560s and then went to Peru, where he remained until 1585. He wrote his account twenty-five years after Aguirre's death, in the hope, he said, of ensuring that the story would not be forgotten, for it had taken place in the Indies 'where there is a lack of writers and people who are curious to enquire into such things'. His chronicle is detailed and sensational, too, in places, as he himself implies when he writes: 'In [this story] you will find cruelty, passion, and incidents arousing great pity . . .'

To set alongside Ortiguera's version there are a number of

eye-witness accounts. These are of great interest, for they come from men who were with Aguirre all the way down the Amazon and who saw everything that happened at close quarters. The fact that they are often badly written, obscure, or unintelligible only adds to their documentary value as the accounts of ordinary men close to extraordinary events.

First, chronologically, from August 1561, come a handful of pages by one of Aguirre's most trusted allies, Pedro de Monguía. A few weeks later comes a short account from Gonzalo de Zúñiga, a chronicler who arrived in the Indies from Seville as a boy of sixteen and who first served under Ursúa in the 1540s. Next there is a short, anonymous account, written not long after Aguirre's death. Of all of them, this is the version which paints the most negative picture of Ursúa's actions and character; it is also the only one to tell us the name of Aguirre's *mestiza* daughter – Elvira.

Dating from 1562, there is another short account. It, too, is technically anonymous, but the fact that a soldier named Custodio Hernández plays so prominent a role in the proceedings suggests that it can only have been written by him.

Much longer than any of these chronicles, and much more carefully written, is that of Francisco Vázquez, which also dates from 1562. His account, subsequently plagiarised by another eye-witness chronicler Pedrarias de Almesto, is the clearest, most detailed, and perhaps the most reliable. It often serves as a guide when there is confusion and disagreement among the rest.

In addition, there are three letters written, or rather dictated, by Aguirre himself. They are fascinating in many ways. Curiously, though they do give an idea of his point of view, they are easily reconcilable with the accounts of others. It's as if, at the end of his unsuccessful life, Aguirre had freely chosen the only role left to him, that of villain of the piece.

Besides these key accounts there are a number of later ones, including a version in English by Robert Southey (1774-1843) – poet laureate and friend of Coleridge – called *The Expedition of Orsua, and the Crimes of Aguirre.* But none of the later accounts tells us anything new.

# BIBLIOGRAPHY

Agurto Calvo, S., *Lima prehispánica*, Lima, 1984.

Arciniega, R., *Dos rebeldes españoles en el Perú: Gonzalo Pizarro . . . y Lope de Aguirre*, Buenos Aires, 1946.

Baudin, L., *La Vie quotidienne au temps des derniers Incas*, Paris, 1955.

—, *A Socialist Empire: The Incas of Peru* (translated from the French), New York, 1961.

Bethell, L. (ed.), *The Cambridge History of Latin America*, Cambridge, 1984-.

Blanco, H., *Land or Death: The Peasant Struggle in Peru* (translated from the Spanish), New York, 1972.

del Busto Duthúrburu, J. A., 'Los "Amazonautas" del siglo XVI', *Revista Histórica*, Lima, 29, 1966, pp. 207-80.

—, *La expedición de Hernando Pizarro a Pachacámac*, Lima, 1967.

del Campo, L., *Pedro de Ursúa: conquistador español del siglo XVI*, Pamplona, 1970.

Canavaggio, J., *Cervantes* (translated from the French), New York and London, 1990.

Caro Baroja, J., *El señor inquisidor y otras vidas por oficio*, Madrid, 1968.

—, *Los vascos*, 3rd edition, Madrid, 1971.

—, *Introducción a la historia social y económica del pueblo vasco*, San Sebastián, 1986.

—, *Vasconiana*, San Sebastián, 1986.

de Carvajal, G., *The Discovery of the Amazon* (translated from the Spanish), New York, 1934.

de Cieza de León, P., *Crónica del Perú*, ed. F. Pease & M. Maticorena, Lima, 1984.

Crosby, A. W., *The Columbian Exchange: Biological and Cultural Consequences of 1492*, Westport, Connecticut, 1972.

Descola, J., *La Vie quotidienne au Pérou au temps des Espagnols, 1710-1820*, Paris, 1962.

Edge, D., & Paddock, J. M., *Arms and Armour of the Medieval Knight*, London, 1988.

Gott, R., *Guerrilla Movements in Latin America*, London, 1970.

Grubb, K. G., *The Lowland Indians of Amazonia*, London, 1927.

Hemming, J., *The Conquest of the Incas*, London, 1970.

—, *Red Gold: The Conquest of the Brazilian Indians*, London, 1978.

—, *Amazon Frontier: The Defeat of the Brazilian Indians*, London, 1987.

Inglis, B., *Roger Casement*, London, 1973.

de Ispizua, S., *Historia de los vascos en el descubrimiento, conquista y civilización de América*, 6 vols, Bilbao, 1914-19.

Jos, E., *Ciencia y osadía sobre Lope de Aguirre el peregrino*, Seville, 1950.

Katz, F., *The Ancient American Civilisations* (translated from the German), London, 1972.

Kauffmann Doig, F., *Manual de arqueología peruana*, 8th edition, Lima, 1983.

Keatinge, R. W. (ed.), *Peruvian Prehistory*, Cambridge, 1988.

Lasso de la Vega, G., *El Inca, Royal Commentaries of the Incas*, 2 vols (translated from the Spanish), Austin, 1966.

Lathrap, D. W., *The Upper Amazon*, London, 1970.

Lockhart, J., *Spanish Peru, 1532-1560*, Madison, 1968.

—, *The Men of Cajamarca*, Austin, 1972.

*Lope de Aguirre descuartizado*, La Academia Errante, San Sebastián, 1963.

López, C. F., *La Margarita*, Caracas, 1940.

—, *Lope de Aguirre el peregrino, primer caudillo de América*, Barcelona, 1953.

Lovett, A. W., *Early Habsburg Spain, 1517-1598*, Oxford, 1986.

Morón, G., *Historia de Venezuela*, 5 vols, Caracas, 1971.

*Navarra: castillos y palacios*, Caja de Ahorros de Navarra, 1980.

Ortiz de Zevallos, A., *Lima a los 450 años*, Lima, 1986.

Ortzi (F. Letamendia Belzunce), *Historia de Euskadi: el nacionalismo vasco y ETA*, Paris, 1975.

Pierson, P., *Philip II of Spain*, London, 1975.

Porras Barrenechea, R., *Mito, tradición e historia del Perú*, Lima, 1951.

Russell, P. E. (ed.), *Spain: A Companion to Spanish Studies*, London, 1973.

Serrano y Sanz, M. (ed.), *Historiadores de Indias*, vol. 2, Madrid, 1909.

Simón, P., *The Expedition of Pedro de Ursúa and Lope de Aguirre* . . . (translated from the Spanish), London, 1861.

Singleton-Gates, P., & Girodias, M., *The Black Diaries: An Account of Roger Casement's Life and Times, with a Collection of his Diaries and Public Writings*, Paris, 1959.

Southey, R., *The Expedition of Orsua; and the Crimes of Aguirre*, London, 1821.

Squier, E. G., *Peru: Incidents of Travel and Exploration in the Land of the Incas*, 2nd edition, London, 1878.

Subero, J. M., *Historia del Estado Nueva Esparta*, Caracas, 1980.

Taylor, L., 'Peru's Alan García: Supplanting the Old Order', *Third World Quarterly*, 8, 1986, pp. 100–36.

Vale, M., *War and Chivalry*, London, 1981.

Valverde, L., *Historia de Guipúzcoa*, San Sebastián, 1984.

Wachtel, N., *La Vision des vaincus: les Indiens du Pérou devant la Conquête espagnole*, Paris, 1971.

Weinstein, B., *The Amazon Rubber Boom, 1850-1920*, Stanford, 1983.

Woodroffe, J. F., *The Upper Reaches of the Amazon*, London, 1914.

Wright, R., *Cut Stones and Crossroads*, Harmondsworth, 1986.

de Zárate, A., *The Discovery and Conquest of Peru* (translated from the Spanish), Harmondsworth, 1968.

For the text of the chronicles of the Aguirre story, I have mostly used the edition of Elena Mampel González and Neus Escandell Tur – *Lope de Aguirre: Crónicas, 1559-1561*, Barcelona, 1981.